1st EDITION

Perspectives on Diseases and Disorders

AIDS

Katherine Macfarlane

Book Editor

GREENHAVEN PRESS

A part of Gale, Cengage Learning

Detroit • New York • San Francisco • New Haven, Conn • Waterville, Maine • London

© 2008 Gale, a part of Cengage Learning

For more information, contact:
Greenhaven Press
27500 Drake Rd.
Farmington Hills, MI 48331-3535
Or you can visit our Internet site at gale.cengage.com

Cover photo: © Gideon Mendel/CORBIS

LIBRARY OF CONGRESS CATALOGING-IN-PUBLICATION DATA

AIDS / Katherine Macfarlane, book editor.
   p. cm. — (Perspectives on diseases and disorders)
Includes bibliographical references and index.
ISBN 13: 978-0-7377-3868-1 (hardcover)
1. AIDS (Disease)—Popular works. I. Macfarlane, Katherine.
RC606.64.A335 2008
616.97'92—dc22

2007037471

ISBN-10: 0-7377-3868-5

Printed in the United States of America
2 3 4 5 6 7 12 11 10 09 08

CONTENTS

CHAPTER 2 Issues Concerning AIDS

INTRODUCTION

Acquired immune deficiency syndrome (AIDS), and the human immunodeficiency virus (HIV) that causes it, have been called "the most serious threat to humankind since the black death."[1] Yet the developed world has been remarkably slow to confront a disease that is now recognized as a pandemic of global and terrifying proportions.

This unresponsiveness was largely due to the way the disease first manifested itself: HIV evolved in sub-Saharan Africa. The developed world was not particularly concerned that black Africans were dying of some exotic tropical plague. As far as the developed world was concerned, Africans were always dying of strange and exotic diseases, and people in the developed world really did not feel that this was their problem. To quote South African Karen Jochelson, they viewed Africa "as a sick and dying continent, harbouring deadly disease and inhabited by an essentially promiscuous people who are part of a dangerous, wild, natural world and bound by primitive traditions and superstitions."[2]

When AIDS left Africa and entered the United States, it initially plagued homosexuals and drug users, which further fueled the idea that AIDS was a disease of "undesirables" and not something to worry about. It was not until it became clear that AIDS was a sexually transmitted disease affecting the general population of the developed world, not just homosexual men and intravenous drug users, that Western scientists began to work seriously on a means of treating and controlling AIDS. The drug AZT (azidothymidine) was approved for use by the Federal Drug Administration in 1987. Although AZT alone proved an unsatisfactory therapy because of debilitating side effects and the capacity of the virus to develop immunity to it, a therapy known as highly active antiretroviral therapy (HAART), which uses new drugs in various combinations both with one another and with AZT, is greatly improving the lives of people infected with the HIV virus.

As of 2007 HIV/AIDS in Africa south of the Sahara desert is a pandemic that is devastating the population, killing young adults in what should be their most productive years, and leaving a generation of children—whose numbers are estimated to reach 25 million by 2010—without parents, guidance, and the very necessities of life. Some sociologists believe that these children, raised with little hope or warmth, may turn to violent insurrection and even terrorism, posing a serious threat to world stability. Says General Charles Wald, the former head of European Command, which oversees U.S. military operations in most of Africa, "Where do you think the next breeding ground for terrorism will be?"[3]

Treatment Is Necessary for All

In the developed world, the poor and uneducated, especially impoverished blacks and Latinos in the United States, are not getting help to treat AIDS. Without health insurance, many are not tested for HIV and are spreading the disease to their sexual partners, both male and female. Because full-blown AIDS can take up to ten years to manifest itself in a person infected with HIV, those infected have many years to spread the disease to multiple partners.

HIV/AIDS has spread to every part of the world. Although the reported incidence of new infections has leveled off or fallen in the developed world, infection in regions of the developing world is increasing rapidly. Wherever the next major epidemic occurs—Russia, the Middle East, India, China, or Southeast Asia—the one

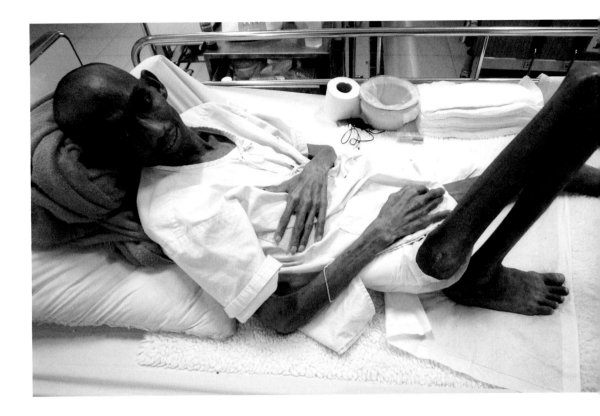

certainty is that AIDS will be both a heterosexual disease and a disease predominantly of women. The reason for this is twofold: Women are twice as likely as men to be infected with HIV by vaginal intercourse, and throughout much of the developing world, women have no control over their own bodies. For a woman to refuse a man his "rights" over her or to insist on the practice of safe sex (using a condom) is to risk being beaten and forced to have sex or being thrown out of her husband's house to live a life of beggary or prostitution. Throughout Africa and much of the rest of the developing world, men see using a condom as an insult to their manhood and refuse even to consider it.

What to do about the HIV/AIDS pandemic is an issue that world leaders are only beginning to confront. HIV has shown itself to be a versatile microorganism. It

A patient with a highly progressed case of AIDS lies in a hospital in central Thailand. (**AP Images**)

mutates rapidly and quickly develops resistance to existing drug therapies.

Still, steps can and must be taken. In the long term, the developed world and the developing world must work together to put an end to poverty and ignorance so that people around the world will have both the knowledge and the means to protect themselves from the disease.

In the short term, the developed world must make the antiretroviral drugs that are containing the disease in the United States and Europe available to the developing world so that young adults can live long enough to bring up their children and provide for their well-being. Ultimately, both the developed world and the developing world must work toward effective HIV vaccines that will immunize people not infected with the virus and also help infected people to withstand the disease.

Notes

1. Charlie Furniss, "AIDS Crisis: Twenty-Five Years On," *Geographical*, January 2006, p. 47.

2. Quoted in Susan S. Hunter, *Black Death: AIDS in Africa*. New York: Palgrave Macmillan, 2003, p. 53.

3. Quoted in Stephan Faris, "Containment Strategy: Iran. North Korea. Uganda? Why the Pentagon Ranks Africa's AIDS Epidemic as a Leading Security Threat," *Atlantic Monthly*, December 2006, p. 34.

CHAPTER 1

Understanding AIDS

AIDS:
An Overview
of the Disease

Rebecca J. Frey and Teresa G. Odle

In the following article, Rebecca J. Frey and Teresa G. Odle define acquired immune deficiency syndrome (AIDS). They explain the disease's means of transmission and discuss its diagnosis and symptoms, including opportunistic infections and other diseases that prey on the patient's depressed immune system. Frey and Odle conclude with a discussion of the prognosis and prevention of the disease.

Rebecca J. Frey is a professional editor and writer who has written extensively on medical subjects. Teresa G. Odle is a writer and editor who has worked in health-care communication for many years and is a member of the American Medical Writers Association.

Photo on previous page. Dr. Mahlon Johnson accidentally infected himself with HIV during an autopsy. Now, he takes a cocktail of drugs to combat the disease: AZT, lamivudine, and protease inhibitors. (Taro Yamasaki/Time & Life Pictures/Getty Images)

Acquired immune deficiency syndrome (AIDS) is an infectious disease caused by the human immunodeficiency virus (HIV). It was first recognized in the United States in 1981. AIDS is the advanced form of infection with the HIV virus, which may not

SOURCE: Rebecca J. Frey and Teresa G. Odle, *The Gale Encyclopedia of Medicine*, Third Edition, Farmington Hills, MI: Gale, 2006. Reproduced by permission of Gale, a part of Cengage Learning.

cause recognizable disease for a long period after the initial exposure (latency). No vaccine is currently available to prevent HIV infection. At present, all forms of AIDS therapy are focused on improving the quality and length of life for AIDS patients by slowing or halting the replication of the virus and treating or preventing infections and cancers that take advantage of a person's weakened immune system. . . .

Risk Factors

AIDS can be transmitted in several ways. The risk factors for HIV transmission vary according to category:

FAST FACT

The virus that causes AIDS is believed to have originated in a chimpanzee subspecies, which passed it on to humans when hunters were exposed to their blood.

- Sexual contact. Persons at greatest risk are those who do not practice safe sex, those who are not monogamous, those who participate in anal intercourse, and those who have sex with a partner with symptoms of advanced HIV infection and/or other sexually transmitted diseases (STDs). In the United States and Europe, most cases of sexually transmitted HIV infection have resulted from homosexual contact, whereas in Africa, the disease is spread primarily through sexual intercourse among heterosexuals.

- Transmission in pregnancy. High-risk mothers include women married to bisexual men or men who have an abnormal blood condition called hemophilia and require blood transfusions, intravenous drug users, and women living in neighborhoods with a high rate of HIV infection among heterosexuals. The chances of transmitting the disease to the child are higher in women in advanced stages of the disease. Breast feeding increases the risk of transmission by 10–20%. The use of zidovudine (AZT) during pregnancy, however, can decrease the risk of transmission to the baby.

• Exposure to contaminated blood or blood products. With the introduction of blood product screening in the mid-1980s, the incidence of HIV transmission in blood transfusions has dropped to one in every 100,000 transfused. With respect to HIV transmission among drug abusers, risk increases with the duration of using injections, the frequency of needle sharing, the number of persons who share a needle, and the number of AIDS cases in the local population.

• Needle sticks among health care professionals. Present studies indicate that the risk of HIV transmission by a needle stick is about one in 250. This rate can be decreased if the injured worker is given AZT, an anti-retroviral medication, in combination with other medication.

HIV is not transmitted by handshakes or other casual non-sexual contact, coughing or sneezing, or by bloodsucking insects such as mosquitoes. . . .

Causes and Symptoms

Because HIV destroys immune system cells, AIDS is a disease that can affect any of the body's major organ systems. HIV attacks the body through three disease processes: immunodeficiency, autoimmunity, and nervous system dysfunction.

Immunodeficiency describes the condition in which the body's immune response is damaged, weakened, or is not functioning properly. In AIDS, immunodeficiency results from the way that the virus binds to a protein called CD4 which is primarily found on the surface of certain subtypes of white blood cells called helper T cells or CD4 cells. After the virus has attached to the CD4 receptor, the virus-CD4 complex refolds to uncover another receptor called a chemokine receptor that helps to mediate entry of the virus into the cell. One chemokine receptor in particular, CCR5, has gotten recent attention after studies

Risk of Acquiring HIV Infection, by Entry Site

Entry Site	Risk Virus Reaches Entry Site	Risk Virus Enters	Risk Inoculated
Eye tissues	Moderate	Moderate	Very low
Tissues of the mouth	Moderate	Moderate	Low
Tissues of the nose	Low	Low	Very low
Lower respiratory	Very low	Very low	Very low
Anus	Very high	Very high	Very high
Skin, intact	Very low	Very low	Very low
Skin, broken	Low	High	High
Penis	High	Low	Low
Vagina	Low	Low	Medium
Ulcers (STD)	High	High	Very high
Blood products (infusions, etc.)	High	High	High
Shared needles	High	High	Very high
Accidental needle	Low	High	Low
Traumatic wound	Modest	High	High
Mother to child	High	High	High

The risk of HIV virus reaching an entry site; the risk that, having reached the entry sight, the virus enters the blood stream; and the risk that the individual is then infected with HIV.

Source: "AIDS." Rebecca J. Frey and Teresa G. Odle, *The Gale Encyclopedia of Medicine*. Third Edition, Jacqueline L. Longe, Editor. 5 vols. Farmington Hills, MI: Thomson Gale, 2006.

showed that defects in its structure (caused by genetic mutations) cause the progression of AIDS to be prevented or slowed. Scientists hope that this discovery will lead to the development of drugs that trigger an artificial mutation of the CCR5 gene or target the CCR5 receptor.

Once HIV has entered the cell, it can replicate intracellularly and kill the cell in ways that are still not completely understood. In addition to killing some lymphocytes directly, the AIDS virus disrupts the functioning of the remaining CD4 cells. Because the immune system cells are destroyed, many different types of infections and cancers that take advantage of a person's weakened immune system (opportunistic) can develop.

Autoimmunity is a condition in which the body's immune system produces antibodies that work against its own cells. Antibodies are specific proteins produced in response to exposure to a specific, usually foreign, protein or particle called an antigen. In this case, the body produces antibodies that bind to blood platelets that are necessary for proper blood clotting and tissue repair. Once bound, the antibodies mark the platelets for removal from the body, and they are filtered out by the spleen. Some AIDS patients develop a disorder, called immune-related thrombocytopenia purpura (ITP), in which the number of blood platelets drops to abnormally low levels.

Researchers do not know precisely how HIV attacks the nervous system since the virus can cause damage without infecting nerve cells directly. One theory is that, once infected with HIV, one type of immune system cell, called a macrophage, begins to release a toxin that harms the nervous system.

The course of AIDS generally progresses through three stages, although not all patients will follow this progression precisely:

Acute Retroviral Syndrome

Acute retroviral syndrome is a term used to describe a group of symptoms that can resemble mononucleosis and that may be the first sign of HIV infection in 50–70% of all patients and 45–90% of women. Most patients are not recognized as infected during this phase and may not seek medical attention. The symptoms may include fever, fatigue, muscle aches, loss of appetite, digestive disturbances, weight loss, skin rashes, headache, and chronically swollen lymph nodes (lymphadenopathy). Approximately 25–33% of patients will experience a form of meningitis during this phase in which the membranes that cover the brain and spinal cord become inflamed. Acute retroviral syndrome develops between one and six weeks after infection, and lasts for two to three weeks. Blood tests during this period will indicate the presence of virus (viremia) and the appearance of the viral p24 antigen in the blood.

Latency Period

After the HIV virus enters a patient's lymph nodes during the acute retroviral syndrome stage, the disease becomes latent for as many as 10 years or more before symptoms of advanced disease develop. During latency, the virus continues to replicate in the lymph nodes, where it may cause one or more of the following conditions:

Persistent Generalized Lymphadenopathy(PGL)

Persistent generalized lymphadenopathy, or PGL, is a condition in which HIV continues to produce chronic painless swellings in the lymph nodes during the latency period. The lymph nodes that are most frequently affected by PGL are those in the areas of the neck, jaw, groin, and armpits. PGL affects between 50-70% of patients during latency.

Constitutional Symptoms

Many patients will develop low-grade fevers, chronic fatigue, and general weakness. HIV may also cause a combination of food malabsorption, loss of appetite, and increased metabolism that contribute to the so-called AIDS wasting or wasting syndrome.

Other Organ Systems

At any time during the course of HIV infection, patients may suffer from a yeast infection in the mouth called thrush, open sores or ulcers, or other infections of the mouth; diarrhea and other gastrointestinal symptoms that cause malnutrition and weight loss; diseases of the lungs and kidneys; and degeneration of the nerve fibers in the arms and legs. HIV infection of the nervous system leads to general loss of strength, loss of reflexes, and feelings of numbness or burning sensations in the feet or lower legs.

Late-Stage Disease (AIDS)

AIDS is usually marked by a very low number of CD4+ lymphocytes, followed by a rise in the frequency of opportunistic infections and cancers. Doctors monitor the number and proportion of CD4+ lymphocytes in the patient's blood in order to assess the progression of the disease and the effectiveness of different medications. About 10% of infected individuals never progress to this overt stage of the disease and are referred to as nonprogressors.

Opportunistic Infections

Once the patient's CD4+ lymphocyte count falls below 200 cells/mm^3 [cubic millimeter], he or she is at risk for a variety of opportunistic infections. The infectious organisms may include the following:

- Fungi. The most common fungal disease associated with AIDS is Pneumocystis carinii pneumonia (PCP). PCP is the immediate cause of death in 15–20% of AIDS patients. It is an important measure of a patient's prognosis. Other fungal infections include a yeast infection of the mouth (candidiasis or thrush) and cryptococcal meningitis.

- Protozoa. Toxoplasmosis is a common opportunistic infection in AIDS patients that is caused by a protozoan. Other diseases in this category include isoporiasis and cryptosporidiosis.

- Mycobacteria. AIDS patients may develop tuberculosis or MAC infections. MAC infections are caused by Mycobacterium avium-intracellulare, and occur in about 40% of AIDS patients. It is rare until CD4+ counts falls below 50 cells/mm^3.

- Bacteria. AIDS patients are likely to develop bacterial infections of the skin and digestive tract.
- Viruses. AIDS patients are highly vulnerable to cytomegalovirus (CMV), herpes simplex virus (HSV), varicella zoster virus (VZV), and Epstein-Barr virus (EBV) infections. Another virus, JC virus, causes progressive destruction of brain tissue in the brain stem, cerebrum, and cerebellum (multifocal leukoencephalopathy or PML), which is regarded as an AIDS-defining illness by the Centers for Disease Control and Prevention [CDC].

AIDS Dementia Complex and Neurologic Complications

AIDS dementia complex is usually a late complication of the disease. It is unclear whether it is caused by the direct effects of the virus on the brain or by intermediate causes. AIDS dementia complex is marked by loss of reasoning ability, loss of memory, inability to concentrate, apathy and loss of initiative, and unsteadiness or weakness in walking. Some patients also develop seizures. There are no specific treatments for AIDS dementia complex.

Musculoskeletal Complications

Patients in late-stage AIDS may develop inflammations of the muscles, particularly in the hip area, and may have arthritis-like pains in the joints.

Oral Symptoms

In addition to thrush and painful ulcers in the mouth, patients may develop a condition called hairy leukoplakia of the tongue. This condition is also regarded by the CDC as an indicator of AIDS. Hairy leukoplakia is a white area of diseased tissue on the tongue that may be flat or slightly raised. It is caused by the Epstein-Barr virus.

AIDS-Related Cancers

Patients with late-stage AIDS may develop Kaposi's sarcoma (KS), a skin tumor that primarily affects homosexual men.

KS is the most common AIDS-related malignancy. It is characterized by reddish-purple blotches or patches (brownish in African-Americans) on the skin or in the mouth. About 40% of patients with KS develop symptoms in the digestive tract or lungs. KS may be caused by a herpes virus—like sexually transmitted disease agent rather than HIV.

The second most common form of cancer in AIDS patients is a tumor of the lymphatic system (lymphoma). AIDS-related lymphomas often affect the central nervous system and develop very aggressively.

Invasive cancer of the cervix (related to certain types of human papilloma virus [HPV]) is an important diagnostic marker of AIDS in women.

While incidence of AIDS-defining cancers such as Kaposi's sarcoma and cervical cancer have decreased since increased use of antiretroviral therapy, other cancers have increased in AIDS patients. People with HIV have shown higher incidence of lung cancer, head and neck cancers, Hodgkin's lymphoma, melanoma, and anorectal cancer from 1992 to 2002.

Diagnosis

Because HIV infection produces such a wide range of symptoms, the CDC has drawn up a list of 34 conditions regarded as defining AIDS. The physician will use the CDC list to decide whether the patient falls into one of these three groups:

- definitive diagnoses with or without laboratory evidence of HIV infection
- definitive diagnoses with laboratory evidence of HIV infection
- presumptive diagnoses with laboratory evidence of HIV infection.

Physical Findings

Almost all the symptoms of AIDS can occur with other diseases. The general physical examination may range from normal findings to symptoms that are closely associated with AIDS. These symptoms are hairy leukoplakia of the tongue and Kaposi's sarcoma. When the doctor examines the patient, he or she will look for the overall pattern of symptoms rather than any one finding.

Laboratory Tests for HIV Infection

The first blood test for AIDS was developed in 1985. At present, patients who are being tested for HIV infection are usually given an enzyme-linked immunosorbent assay (ELISA) test for the presence of HIV antibody in their blood. Positive ELISA results are then tested with a Western blot or immunofluorescence (IFA) assay for confirmation. The combination of the ELISA and Western blot tests is more than 99.9% accurate in detecting HIV infection within four to eight weeks following exposure. The polymerase chain reaction (PCR) test can be used to detect the presence of viral nucleic acids in the very small number of HIV patients who have false-negative results on the ELISA and Western blot tests. These tests are also used to detect viruses and bacterium other than HIV and AIDS.

In addition to diagnostic blood tests, there are other blood tests that are used to track the course of AIDS in patients that have already been diagnosed. These include blood counts, viral load tests, p24 antigen assays, and measurements of 22-microglobulin (22M).

Doctors will use a wide variety of tests to diagnose the presence of opportunistic infections, cancers, or other disease conditions in AIDS patients. Tissue biopsies, samples of cerebrospinal fluid, and sophisticated imaging techniques, such as magnetic resonance imaging (MRI) and computed tomography scans (CT) are used to diagnose AIDS-related cancers, some opportunistic infections, damage to the central nervous system, and wasting of the muscles. Urine and stool samples are used to diagnose infections caused by parasites. AIDS patients are also given blood tests for syphilis and other sexually transmitted diseases.

Diagnosis in Children

Diagnostic blood testing in children older than 18 months is similar to adult testing, with ELISA screening confirmed by Western blot. Younger infants can be diagnosed by direct culture of the HIV virus, PCR testing, and p24 antigen testing.

In terms of symptoms, children are less likely than adults to have an early acute syndrome. They are, however, likely to have delayed growth, a history of frequent illness, recurrent ear infections, a low blood cell count, failure to gain weight, and unexplained fever. Children with AIDS are more likely to develop bacterial infections, inflammation of the lungs, and AIDS-related brain disorders than are HIV-positive adults. . . .

Prognosis

At the present time, there is no cure for AIDS.

Treatment stresses aggressive combination drug therapy for those patients with access to the expensive medications and who tolerate them adequately. The use of these multi-drug therapies has significantly reduced the numbers of deaths, in this country, resulting from AIDS. The data is still inconclusive, but the potential exists to possibly prolong life indefinitely using these and other drug therapies to boost the immune system, keep the virus from replicating, and ward off opportunistic infections and malignancies.

Prognosis after the latency period depends on the patient's specific symptoms and the organ systems affected by the disease. Patients with AIDS-related lymphomas of the central nervous system die within two to three months of diagnosis; those with systemic lymphomas may survive for eight to ten months.

Prevention

As of 2005, there was no vaccine effective against AIDS. Several vaccines are currently being investigated, however, both to prevent initial HIV infection and as a therapeutic treatment to prevent HIV from progressing to full-blown AIDS.

In the meantime, there are many things that can be done to prevent the spread of AIDS:

- Being monogamous and practice safe sex. Individuals must be instructed in the proper use of condoms

This artist's depiction portrays the human immunodeficiency virus (right) about to infect a human T cell. (3D4Medical.com/Getty Images)

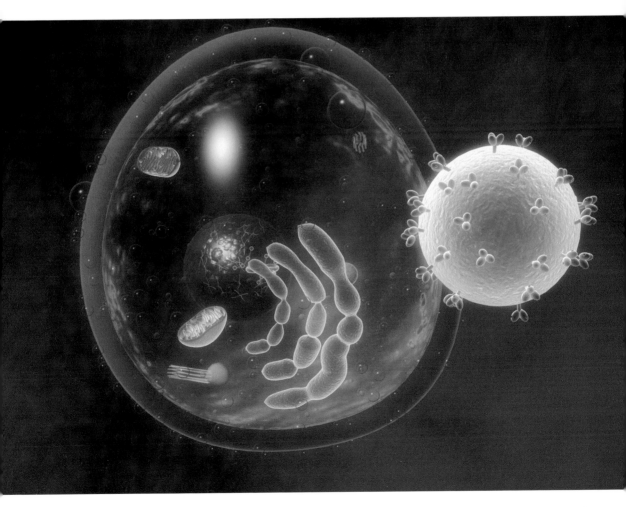

and urged to practice safe sex. Besides avoiding the risk of HIV infection, condoms are successful in preventing other sexually transmitted diseases and unwanted pregnancies. Before engaging in a sexual relationship with someone, getting tested for HIV infection is recommended.

• Avoiding needle sharing among intravenous drug users.

• Although blood and blood products are carefully monitored, those individuals who are planning to undergo major surgery may wish to donate blood ahead of time to prevent a risk of infection from a blood transfusion.

• Healthcare professionals must take all necessary precautions by wearing gloves and masks when handling body fluids and preventing needle-stick injuries.

• If someone suspects HIV infection, he or she should be tested for HIV. If treated aggressively and early, the development of AIDS may be postponed indefinitely. If HIV infection is confirmed, it is also vital to let sexual partners know so that they can be tested and, if necessary, receive medical attention.

Current Drug Therapies for AIDS

ehealthMD

The U.S. Food and Drug Administration has approved a number of anti-retroviral drugs as part of the most recent strategy against HIV/AIDS. These drugs in various combinations (known as "cocktails") compose the highly active antiretroviral therapy that is making it possible for people infected with HIV to live longer and enjoy better health. New drugs are also available to treat the opportunistic diseases that take advantage of AIDS victims' weakened immune systems.

ehealthMD is a product of Health Information Publications, a company specializing in health information delivered over the Internet.

When AIDS first surfaced in the United States, no drugs were available to combat the underlying immune deficiency, and few treatments existed for the opportunistic infections that resulted. Over the past 10 years, however, therapies have been developed to fight both HIV infection and its associated infections and cancers.

SOURCE: "What Treatments Are Available for HIV and AIDS?" www.ehealthMD.com, January 2004. Reproduced by permission.

What Treatments Are Available for HIV and AIDS?

Although there is no treatment currently available that can cure people of HIV or AIDS, a number of therapies have been developed to help them stay healthier and live longer.

- Some medications target HIV itself, to reduce the virus's assault on the immune system.
- Other treatments are used to treat or prevent specific opportunistic infections that threaten the health of people with HIV-damaged immune systems.

Treatments That Suppress HIV

Drugs that interfere with the activity of a retrovirus such as HIV are generally known as antiretrovirals. All antiretroviral medications currently approved to treat HIV infection target two viral enzymes used by the virus to replicate itself. These enzymes, reverse transcriptase and protease, are involved in different stages of viral replication.

Three classes of antiretroviral drugs have been developed to interfere with the activity of these viral enzymes and slow down the multiplication of the virus. These are:

- Nucleoside analog reverse transcriptase inhibitors (NRTIs). NRTIs interrupt an early stage of HIV replication by interfering with the activity of reverse transcriptase. AZT (zidovudine), the first drug approved for treating HIV infection, is an NRTI, as are zalcitabine (ddC), didanosine (ddl), stavudine (d4T), lemivudine (3TC), and abacavir.
- Non-nucleoside reverse transcriptase inhibitors (NNRTIs). NNRTIs also work by hindering the action of reverse transcriptase. This class of drugs includes delavirdine, nevirapine, and efavirenz.
- Protease inhibitors. Protease inhibitors interrupt a later stage of viral replication. This class of drugs

includes saquinavir, indinavir, ritonavir, nelfinavir, and amprenavir.

Studies have found that various combinations of antiretroviral drugs are more effective in suppressing HIV than antiretroviral drugs used alone. Experts refer to one common treatment approach, usually involving a protease inhibitor combined with two other antiretroviral drugs, as "highly active antiretroviral therapy" or HAART.

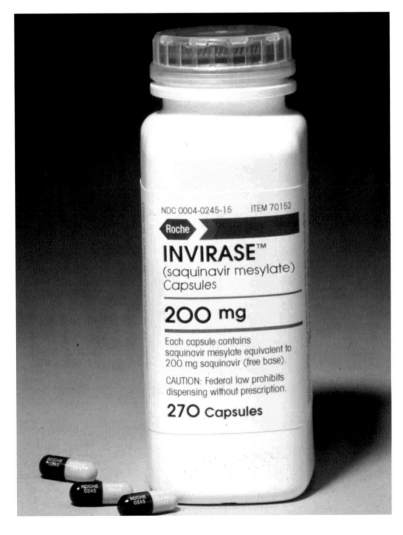

Invirase is a brand name for saquinavir, one of the protease inhibitor class of HIV/AIDS drugs. **(AP Images)**

Drug combinations, or drug "cocktails," also can help reduce the risk that drug-resistant HIV will develop. When drug resistance occurs, medications that initially succeeded in suppressing the replication of HIV in the patient's body lose their effectiveness.

Antiretroviral drugs have side effects that can limit their use in some people.

- AZT, for example, may result in a loss of blood cells.

- Protease inhibitors can cause nausea, diarrhea, and other symptoms.

Treating AIDS-Related Conditions

Other drugs and therapies are used to prevent or treat opportunistic infections and other AIDS-related conditions:

- Pneumocystis carinii pneumonia. People who develop this lung infection are generally treated with TMP/SMX (a combination of antibiotic drugs) or pentamidine. Doctors also prescribe these medications as preventive therapy for adult patients whose CD4+ T cell counts fall below 200.

- Yeast infections in women. Physicians often prescribe a drug called fluconazole to treat yeast and other fungal infections. Fluconazole also can safety prevent vaginal and esophageal candidiasis without development of drug resistance.

- Severe skin ulcers caused by herpes simplex virus infection. Skin ulcers sometimes respond to an antiviral medication, acyclovir.

- Pelvic inflammatory disease. PID is treated with antibiotics. Women with mild cases may be treated on an outpatient basis. HIV-positive pregnant women suspected of having PID are usually hospitalized, treated with intravenous antibiotics approved for use during pregnancy, and monitored closely.

- HIV-related wasting. Megastrol acetate (Megace) is often prescribed for HIV-associated wasting, but it can cause significant irregular bleeding in women. Another drug, nandrolone, may not have these side effects and is currently undergoing drug trials.

- Kaposi's sarcoma and other cancers. Cancers are treated with radiation, chemotherapy, or injections of alpha interferon, a genetically engineered, naturally occurring protein.

What Are Some of the Problems with AIDS Drug Therapy?

AIDS drugs do not cure the condition, but they help to manage it and postpone life-threatening complications. However, there are problems with AIDS drug therapy:

- Side effects of drugs are a major concern in treatment.

- Another major problem is the cost of the drugs used in treating AIDS. AIDS patients in the United States depend on insurance and government grants to obtain them. The high price of these drugs makes it difficult for third-world countries, which have major AIDS epidemics, to afford to distribute them.

Since antiviral drugs have so far not been curative, the hope is to find a vaccine. The technology for vaccine development is present, and serious efforts are being made to find one.

How Can the Psychological Impact of AIDS Be Managed?

When people learn they have tested positive for the HIV virus, they may experience a number of stressful

Drugs Approved for HAART

Nucleoside/Nucleotide RT Inhibitors	Non-Nucleoside RT Inhibitors	Protease Inhibitors	Fusion Inhibitors
Retrovir (zidovudine, AZT)*	Viramune (Nevirapine)*	Invirase (saquinavir-HGC)	Fuzeon (enfuvirtide)*
Videx (didanosine, ddI)*	Receptor (delavirdine)	Norvir (ritonavir)*	
Hivid (zalcitabine, ddC)	Sustiva (efavirenz)*	Crixivan (indinavir)	
Zerit (stavudine, d4T)		Viracept (nelfinavir)*	
Epivir (lamivudine, 3TC)		Fortovase (saquinavir-SGC)	
Combivir (AZT and 3TC)		Agenerase (amprenavir)*	
Ziagen (abacavir)*		Kaletra (lopinavir and ritonavir)*	
Trizivir (AZT + 3TC + abacavir)		Lexiva (fosamprenavir)	
Viread (tenofovir)		Aptivus (tipranavir)	
Emtriva (emtricitabine)		Reyataz (atazanavir)	
Epzicom (abacavir/lamivudine)			
Truvada (tenofovir/emtricitabine)			

*Pediatric approved

Drugs approved for highly active antiretroviral therapy (HAART) of HIV/AIDS, as of April 2006.

Source: "Treatment of HIV Infection," www.niaid.nih.gov/factsheets/treat-hiv.htm (April 2006).

psychological reactions. Depression and anxiety leading to panic attacks may require the help of an adviser or psychological therapist. Counseling services are available in most HIV clinics. Group therapy sessions with other HIV-positive people may also be helpful in managing feelings of stress and guilt.

PERSPECTIVES ON DISEASES AND DISORDERS

People with AIDS who show signs and symptoms of organic central nervous system involvement, such as confusion and memory loss, need particular support. In their cases there is a need for additional medical and psychiatric intervention.

Antidepressant drugs should be used under the advice of a specialist in case of a severe depressive episode. HIV-infected people may take antidepressant drugs, but they are usually more sensitive to their side effects.

Progress on an AIDS Vaccine

National Institute of Allergy and Infectious Diseases

The following National Institute of Allergy and Infectious Diseases (NIAID) fact sheet explains that although vaccines for HIV/AIDS are still in the experimental stages, research is going forward in two directions: vaccines that prevent people from becoming infected by the HIV virus, and vaccines that will boost the immune response of those already infected by the virus.

The NIAID is a branch of the National Institutes of Health. It conducts and supports basic and applied research to understand, treat, and prevent infectious, immunologic, and allergic diseases.

HIV vaccines are aimed at teaching the immune system how to win the battle against HIV. Two types of vaccines can help fight the disease.

• Preventive vaccines aim to generate HIV-specific memory in the immune systems of uninfected persons. Upon contact with the virus, this memory mounts a

SOURCE: "Design of HIV Vaccines," *National Institute of Allergy and Infectious Disease* (NIAID), May 2007.

swift and effective response that prevents HIV from establishing infection. The current generation of preventive vaccines also aims to lower the ability of individuals who do become infected to transmit the virus.

• Therapeutic vaccines are meant to stimulate a potent immune response in people already infected with HIV to help control the infection.

HIV is genetically agile, changing its DNA sequence rapidly to stay ahead of the body's immune response to the virus. To design vaccines, scientists have identified important targets on HIV and on infected human cells. For example, glycoprotein 120 (gp120) on the outer coat or envelope of the virus contains the CD4 binding site, the region that attaches to human cells. Because a large part of gp120 does not mutate but stays constant, vaccines based on genetically engineered HIV envelope proteins gp120 and a larger molecule, gp160, have been tested in clinical trials as possible preventive vaccines. Unfortunately, such vaccines have not been successful in protecting against HIV infection, in part because of the large complex cloak of sugar molecules on the viral coat.

HIV vaccine research has broadened its early focus on HIV envelope proteins and the role of antibodies to include the role of cytotoxic T lymphocytes (CTLs), specific white blood cells that kill infected cells. Researchers are pursuing many novel vaccine strategies that result in production of both anti-HIV antibodies and CTLs. The goal of these approaches is to elicit broad and powerful immune responses that may be the key to developing an effective vaccine.

HIV vaccine candidates are carefully examined by the National Institutes of Health (NIH) and the Food and Drug Administration (FDA) so that the products included in the vaccine cannot cause HIV infection or other severe reactions in humans. The vaccine strategies include

- *Component (or subunit) vaccine:* a structural piece of HIV, such as the outer surface proteins, gp160 or gp120, or a regulatory protein, produced by genetic engineering.

- *Live vector vaccine:* a live bacterium or virus such as vaccinia (used in the smallpox vaccine) modified so it cannot cause disease but can transport a gene that makes one or more HIV proteins into the body.

- *Vaccine combination:* the use of more than one vaccine in a vaccination strategy. For example, use of a

A sex worker in the Dominican Republic prepares to be injected with an experimental AIDS vaccine as part of a clinical trial.
(**AP Images**)

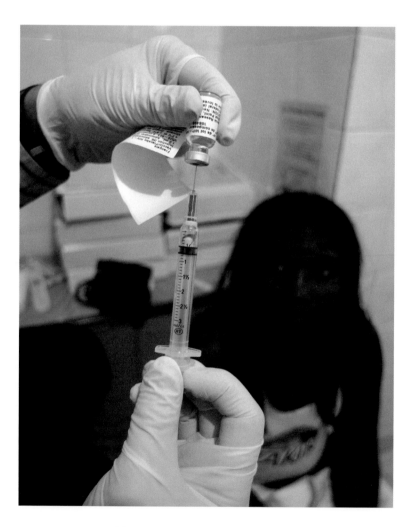

recombinant vector vaccine to induce cellular immune responses followed by booster shots of a component vaccine to stimulate antibody production is a vaccine combination referred to as a prime-boost strategy.

- *Peptide vaccine:* chemically synthesized pieces of HIV proteins (peptides) known to stimulate HIV-specific immunity.
- *Virus-like particle vaccine (pseudovirion vaccine):* a non-infectious HIV look-alike that has one or more, but not all, HIV proteins.
- *DNA vaccine:* a vaccine injected directly into the body that contains genes coding for HIV proteins.

Although vaccines traditionally have been made from whole-killed or live-attenuated virus, no HIV vaccine candidates today are made from these approaches because of safety concerns.

- *Whole-killed virus vaccine:* virus that has been inactivated by chemicals, irradiation, or other means so it is not infectious.
- *Live-attenuated virus vaccine:* live virus from which one or more disease-promoting genes of the virus have been deleted.

Mechanisms to Deliver HIV Vaccines into the Human Body

The human body marshals two defensive measures to combat infectious diseases: antibodies that seek and destroy specific foreign entities in the body, and CTLs. Combinations of different vaccines represent an effective way to enhance the immune responses to HIV. Researchers may first prepare, or "prime," the immune

FAST FACT

An army research institute has revealed that a vaccine is being developed that combines a protein of the anthrax bacterium and one of HIV, and this combination may help prevent infection by intensifying the immune system.

system with one vaccine, such as a live vector vaccine (HIV genes piggybacked onto bacterium or non-HIV virus rendered harmless to serve as delivery systems), and then "boost" the subsequent immune response with a different vaccine, such as a gp120 or gp160 subunit recombinant vaccine.

Several experimental recombinant live vector vaccines made from poxviruses, such as canarypox and modified vaccinia Ankara (MVA), are in clinical trials. These do not reproduce in human cells, and therefore are safe for use. Another example of a vector under development for HIV vaccines is Salmonella, a bacterium that infects the human gut. Scientists also are evaluating DNA vaccines, which are direct injections of genes coding for specific

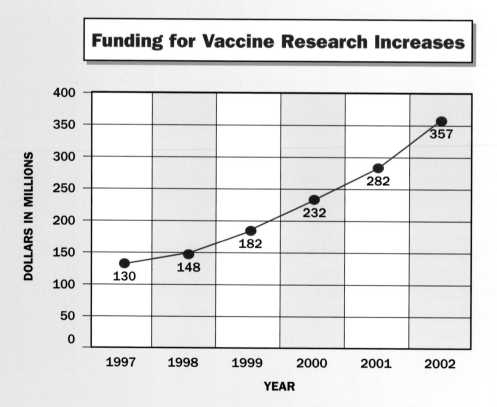

Funding for Vaccine Research Increases

Source: Jack Whitescarver. Department of Health and Human Services.
www.oar.nih.gov/public/pubs/jwfy2002test.htm.

HIV proteins, and have been shown to induce cellular immune responses in human clinical trials. When the DNA is injected, the encoded viral proteins, such as HIV gp160, are produced just as with live vectors.

The National Institute of Allergy and Infectious Diseases Dale and Betty Bumpers Vaccine Research Center has developed an experimental HIV vaccine administered as DNA prime, adenoviral boost expressing HIV genes from three subtypes of HIV—A, B, and C—that together cause about 90 percent of incident HIV infections around the world. The Phase II study of this vaccine was launched in September 2005 in collaboration with the HIV Vaccine Trials Network, the International AIDS Vaccine Initiative, and the U.S. Military HIV Research Program at domestic and international clinical sites. Pre-existing immunity to certain vectors, such as adenovirus, from prior immunizations may blunt the desired immune response to an HIV vaccine. Thus, research is also under way to design alternative adenoviral vector serotypes for which pre-existing immunity is low or absent.

Scientists have found that including certain biologic products, known as adjuvants, in the vaccine preparations can help enhance the strength and durability of immune responses evoked by the vaccine. An adjuvant may work well with one experimental vaccine but not another. FDA therefore licenses the combination, rather than the adjuvant alone. Currently, only one adjuvant, alum, first discovered in 1926, is incorporated into vaccines licensed for human use by FDA. Due to alum's limited activity, however, other adjuvants are under evaluation in animal models and human studies that may be better suited for the newer candidate HIV vaccines.

AIDS: Past, Present, and Future

Susan S. Hunter

HIV/AIDS has struck most cruelly in the part of the world least capable of dealing with it, claims author Susan S. Hunter in the following excerpt. From sub-Saharan Africa, where it is already epidemic, it has spread worldwide and is most prevalent in the developing world, particularly India, eastern Asia, and Russia. Its greatest death toll is among productive young adults in their twenties and thirties, who leave parentless and unsupported children and deprive their countries of the labor needed to produce food and other necessities. Hunter contends that these orphaned children, starving and unsocialized, could cause an increase in crime, civil disorder, and terrorism.

Susan S. Hunter is a medical anthropologist who has worked on AIDS issues in developing countries. She has also worked with the UN Children's Fund, the Joint UN Programme on HIV/AIDS, and the U.S. Agency for International Development. Her books on AIDS have received critical acclaim.

The creative tension of scientific competition and collaboration has been as important in advancing the science of HIV/AIDS as it was to the spinning of evolutionary theory in Darwin's day. In only twenty years, since the first AIDS case was diagnosed in 1982, scientists identified the human immunodeficiency virus (HIV) responsible for autoimmune deficiency disease, or AIDS, developed blood tests to diagnose the disease, and engineered treatments to extend the life of the infected. This is the first time we have had the capacity to watch a massive, global disease event unfold before our very eyes and the first time we had the means to change an epidemic's course before it became a global scourge. Although repeated waves of many other diseases— plague, influenza, tuberculosis, cholera, syphilis —have swept the world since the turn of the twentieth century, HIV/AIDS is the first epidemic of a totally new disease since the 1400s. It is the first global epidemic to begin after medicine crossed the threshold to modernity in the 1950s, gaining the laboratory capability to identify a disease and its causes quickly, the field capacity to prevent its spread, and the data systems needed to track epidemic growth virtually as it occurs. HIV/AIDS is the leading infectious disease threat in the world today, outpacing the two next most important infectious diseases, tuberculosis and malaria, two to one. Not only is it the leading killer in many developing countries, but in the early 1990s it established an early lead over older diseases to become the leading cause of death among eighteen- to thirty-four-year-olds in the United States, where it is now the third leading cause of death among all age groups and rising once again.

HIV, the virus that causes AIDS after lying quiet in an individual for seven to ten years, currently infects 42 million people worldwide. By the end of 2002, the disease had already killed 28 million people, and an estimated 3 million people now die from the disease each year. This is

A grave digger works in the Mbudzi cemetery in Harare, Zimbabwe. Harare is one of many African cities that has been forced to expand its cemeteries to accommodate deaths due to AIDS. (**AP Images**)

8,200 per day, almost three times the number who died in the World Trade Center attack on September 11, 2001. In total, more than 70 million people worldwide have been infected by HIV since the first cases were recorded in 1982 and at least 5 million additional people are being infected each year—some 15,000 per day. If these rates remain the same through the first decade of the twenty-first century, at least 52 million people will have died by 2010 and 58 million will be alive but infected with the virus.

It is likely, given recent reports of infected blood transfusions in China and the HIV mushroom cloud in India and Russia, that global infection rates will soar even higher. An assessment by the U.S. National Intelligence Council in September 2002 warns that the infected populations of five countries alone—Nigeria, Ethiopia, Russia, India, and China—will be 75 million by 2010. If they are added to the existing global HIV reservoir, by 2010 at the very minimum 130 million people will be "incubators walking around with this virus, spreading it to other people," according to Gary Nable, director of the U.S. Vaccine Research Center. Environmentalists warn that South Africa, where one-fifth of adults are HIV-positive, is facing a cemetery crisis and environmental disaster because more than 3 million bodies must be buried over the next ten years. The country's Town and Regional Planning Commission says that with 16,000 people dying each day countrywide, the equivalent of 3,240 football fields will be needed to accommodate the dead in Kwa Zulu Natal Province alone.

> **FAST FACT**
>
> AIDS has killed more than 25 million people, and more than twice that number are living with HIV or AIDS as of 2007.

AIDS surpassed the Black Death's total carnage of 25 million in Europe by the end of 2001 but has not yet topped the *global* death toll from the Black Death, which swept across China, India, the Middle East, and northern Africa before it tainted the wind in Florence in 1347, killing one-quarter to one-half of the inhabitants of every world region except the Americas. It will do so by 2010, when the AIDS death toll will also easily surpass the world's next largest historical disease catastrophe, the depopulation of the Americas in the early 1500s. HIV/AIDS is at least ten times deadlier than any war on the planet and will soon outdistance any of the world's most deadly twentieth-century conflicts. World War I and II together killed 60 million people, the war in Vietnam, 5.1 million combatants and civilians, and the conflict in Korea, 2.4 million. By 2010, if HIV rates remain the same, AIDS will take almost as many lives as those conflicts *plus* the U.S. Civil War, the Bolshevik Revolution, the first Chinese communist war, the Spanish Civil War, the Taiping

Rebellion, the Great War in La Plata, and the partition of India put together.

If we count those who are dying *each day*, AIDS is three times more deadly than terrorism. If we count total number infected *each day*, it is five times more lethal. The disease is a pervasive security threat because it leads to growing poverty, food insecurity, economic and social collapse, deaths among the armed forces and police, increased criminal violence, and sudden power imbalances. In 1990 Kenneth Kaunda, then Zambian president, told a visiting U.S. Congressman that he did not know what he would do when the population of street children in that country's capital, Lusaka, reached 500,000 because the roaming bands of uneducated and unsocialized orphans would become uncontrollable. The U.S. Central Intelligence Agency called AIDS a security threat in 1999, and in January 2001 a National Intelligence Counsel report warned of massive loss of military capabilities and a 20 percent drop in sub-Saharan Africa's gross domestic product (GDP) in less than ten years. Countries in the region may not be able to uphold their peacekeeping commitments on the continent because of mounting deaths. In reverse, of course, war, chaos, economic uncertainty, and social disruption create the perfect conditions for rapid disease spread.

The problem is not just in Africa. From a handful of cases reported in the United States, Europe, and Africa in the early 1980s, AIDS has spread to millions of people in every country of the world. When it first developed, many parts of the world were "clean." By 1993 Poland, countries in Southeast Asia, and Greenland—formerly "clean" areas—reported infections, and by the turn of the twenty-first century there was not an infection-free state in the world. HIV/AIDS is fast becoming the biggest disease burden in the world. Measured by premature death, loss of human potential, disability, and by diminishing capacity and siphoning off· scarce resources,

HIV/AIDS creates losses for everyone, infected or not. Disastrous socioeconomic consequences are predicted for Eurasia as well. The American Enterprise Institute's Nicholas Eberstadt projects huge death tolls, failed economic growth, and dangerous political imbalances in China, India, and Russia by 2025 as a result of AIDS.

Global drag is created because in countries where 20 to 40 percent of the population is infected and 60 percent of new infections occur in people under age twenty-four, AIDS not only kills the most productive people in a society, but they pull others down with them as they slowly and inexorably die. HIV/AIDS deaths and illnesses create huge demographic gaps and vast political, economic, and

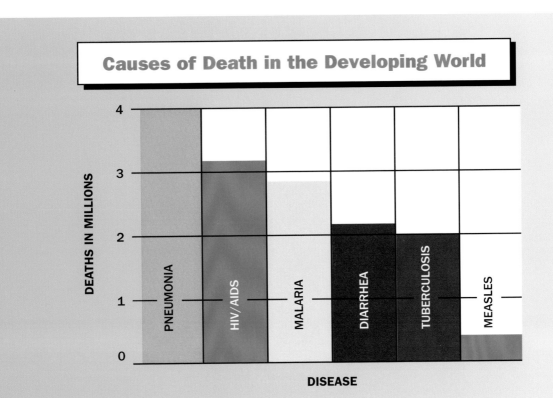

Causes of Death in the Developing World

DEATHS IN MILLIONS

PNEUMONIA HIV/AIDS MALARIA DIARRHEA TUBERCULOSIS MEASLES

DISEASE

According to the World Health Organization, these are the leading killers in the developing world, as of 2004.

Source: Charlie Furniss, "AIDS Crisis: 25 Years On," *Geographical*, January 2006 p. 47.

social problems while it kills off the very people who can address them. The growing food crisis in southern Africa over the past few years is due in large part to HIV/AIDS, which has reduced productivity while increasing the number of desperate individuals who are willing to violate social rules to get food and meet other social needs. Recent food emergencies in that region have put 14.4 million people at risk of starvation, in part because 7 million agricultural workers have died from AIDS since 1985.

AIDS in the Developing World

Charlie Furniss

According to author Charlie Furniss in the following article, AIDS is now becoming recognized as a world health crisis as severe as the Black Death was in the 1300s. By 2010, writes Furniss, the AIDS epidemic in Africa could lead to the collapse of governments, the breakdown of society, famine, widespread crime, chaos, and terrorism. Elsewhere in the developing world, the numbers of HIV cases are rising at an alarming rate. Meanwhile, in the developed world, the rate of infection has stabilized or is dropping. This disparity, the author concludes, is due equally to stigma, denial, and poverty among the people of the developing world and racism and politics in the developed world.

Charlie Furniss is an investigative journalist who has written extensively for *Geographical*.

Thursday 3 October 2002, just another autumn day in Washington DC. But for those meeting at the Centre for Strategic and International Studies

SOURCE: Charlie Furniss, "AIDS Crisis: 25 Years On," *Geographical*, vol. 78, January 2006, pp. 47–52. Copyright © 2006 Circle Publishing Ltd. Reproduced by permission.

(CSIS), it was anything but normal. That morning, more than 40 representatives of the UN, the World Bank, the US National Intelligence Council and various governments and international organisations gathered at the CSIS headquarters at 1800 K Street to discuss the most serious threat to international security known to humankind: not Saddam Hussein, not Osama bin Laden, not even al-Qaeda, but HIV/AIDS.

At that stage, the UN estimated that there were 37.8 million people living with HIV around the world, 25 million of them in sub-Saharan Africa. But delegates were shocked to learn that by 2010, the number of new infections could have topped 100 million, and that a "second wave" of infections in only five countries would dwarf what had so far been seen in Southern Africa. China and India were set to become the new hotspots, with up to 25 million and 15 million new infections respectively, and Nigeria, Russia and Ethiopia would together account for a further 35 million.

In the face of such predictions, HIV/AIDS could no longer be regarded as a purely moral and humanitarian crisis, the delegates were told. In a world where the links between chaos, state failure and "extra-national violence" were increasingly clear, it now had to be considered as a structural and security issue. In Africa, the decimation of civil services threatened to destroy community and social cohesion, while prevalence within the military forces —in some cases as high as 90 per cent—would open doors for chaos and violence.

The death of 16 million agricultural workers in sub-Saharan Africa by 2020 would cause food shortages and malnutrition and subsequently a vicious circle of poverty, disease and death. And the creation of 42 million orphans by 2010 would create a reservoir of rootless, uneducated, un-nurtured young people, "a lost

> **FAST FACT**
>
> Ninety-five percent of all HIV-infected individuals live in developing countries.

generation of potential recruits for crime, military war-lords and terrorists."

Three Years Later

Three years on, and the situation has declined further. According to new UNAIDS [the Joint UN Programme on HIV/AIDS] statistics released last November [2005], more than 40 million people are now HIV+. New epidemics are emerging across Asia and Eastern Europe. Even in North America and Western Europe, new infections among some populations are once more on the rise. UNAIDS warns that if current trends continue, there could be almost 90 million new infections in Africa by 2025, and increasing death rates will cause the populations of seven African countries to drop by more than a third.

But how did it come to this? It's 25 years since the first case of AIDS was diagnosed. And 20 years since it was first identified as a global health issue. In that time, the world has changed beyond recognition, with numerous technological and cultural revolutions altering the everyday lives of people around the globe.

So why do most of the world's young people still have no access to adequate HIV prevention services? Why are 85 per cent of those in need of anti-retroviral therapy (ART) in the developing world still not receiving treatment? And what chance is there now of controlling the 21st century's biggest scourge? . . .

AIDS Worldwide

The HIV/AIDS pandemic shows no sign of abating. According to UNAIDS, 40.3 million people are now living with HIV. Last year alone, there were 4.9 million new infections, and 3.1 million people died of AIDS.

In global terms, HIV/AIDS remains concentrated in sub-Saharan Africa. Home to ten per cent of the world's population, the region contains 65 per cent of all people living with HIV and 77 per cent of infected women. But it's far from a homogeneous pandemic: prevalence varies widely. In East Africa, it has stabilized at around ten per cent, and in West and Central Africa, it has generally not risen above five per cent.

Infection levels are highest in Southern Africa. In eight countries, prevalence is more than 15 per cent, and in Swaziland, Lesotho, Botswana and Namibia it's more than 30 per cent. Because this epidemic is relatively new—breaking out during the early 1990s, ten years after those elsewhere in sub-Saharan Africa—rates are still increasing in such countries as Swaziland and Mozambique.

There is, however, evidence of declining prevalence in several countries. In Uganda, the government has successfully reduced levels from 13 per cent in the early

Relatives visit AIDS patients at the Tambaram Sanitarium near Madras, India. **(AP Images)**

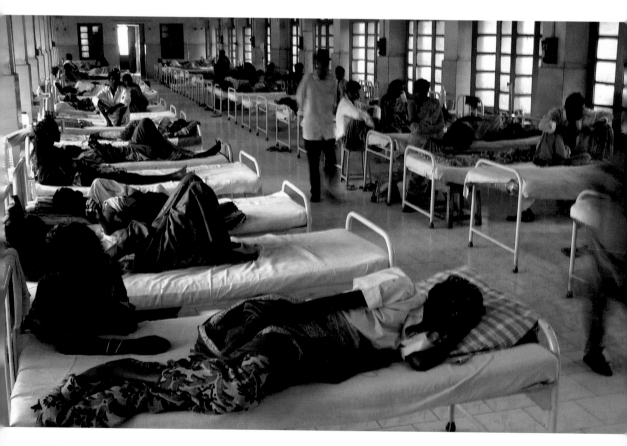

1990s to 4.1 per cent by the end of 2003 through a sustained and effective public-information campaign. There has been a similar drop in Senegal and there are signs that rates may also be decreasing in Kenya.

New Epidemics

But new epidemics are taking hold in East and Central Asia and Eastern Europe. There they tend to be concentrated among certain groups: injecting drug users (IDUs), sex workers and men who have sex with men. Prevalence rates among IDUs in Indonesia, for example, increased from 16 to 48 per cent between 1999 and 2003, and there has been similar growth in China, Vietnam and Nepal. Levels among IDUs have also risen sharply in the Baltic States, Azerbaijan and Uzbekistan, as well as in Russia and Ukraine, although, especially in these last two, commercial sex work has also contributed.

The fear is that members of these groups will transmit HIV to their partners and initiate a more generalized epidemic. Indeed, this has already happened in some areas. In Ukraine, the proportion of new infections from heterosexual transmission rose from 11 per cent in 1997 to 30 per cent in 2003.

Will these epidemics escalate in the way that they have in Africa? Peter Ghys, manager of UNAIDS's epidemic and monitoring team, isn't sure. Outside South Africa, India has the highest number of people living with HIV—more than 5.1 million, mostly living in the country's south. But there, Ghys says, prevalence rates among the general population have remained stable at about one to two per cent since the late 1990s. This fact offers a ray of light. "Epidemic curves from many sub-Saharan African countries show a steep rise and then stabilization," Ghys says. "None have shown stability over a long period at a low prevalence and then risen from that."

Elsewhere, the number of new cases is more or less stable. Outside Africa, some of the highest prevalence rates are in the Caribbean, where the virus is mostly concentrated among sex workers, although it has spilled over into the general population. In Latin America, prevalence varies between 0.1 per cent in Bolivia and 2.5 per cent in Guyana. It tends to be concentrated among injecting drug users in South America and commercial sex workers in Central America, and among men who have sex with men in both regions. In high-income countries, prevalence is stable overall, although in some—particularly the UK, the USA and Germany—numbers of infections are rising among men who have sex with men.

The Effect of the AIDS Epidemic on Children

UNAIDS estimates that HIV/AIDS disease has created 15 million orphans worldwide. Its effect on sub-Saharan Africa is being likened to that of the plague on mediaeval Europe. In Botswana, Swaziland, Zambia and Zimbabwe, life expectancy is less than 35 years, and if current trends persist, the populations of seven Southern African countries will drop by more than a third in the next 20 years. But it isn't just a matter of numbers. HIV primarily affects young adults—last year, almost half of new infections were in young people aged 15 to 24—particularly women. This distortion of population structure is damaging the ability of states to function, says Dr Tom Ellman, medical advisor to MSF [Médecins Sans Frontières] UK. "HIV kills the productive members of society who maintain the social and economic viability of communities."

The threat to key workers is now a particular concern. The Council on Foreign Relations in New York recently warned that HIV/AIDS may foment unrest and undermine state authority. Not only is it weakening military and police forces, it said, but some governments are creating widespread social alienation by prioritizing the treatment of critical officials in an attempt to keep the machinery of the state functioning.

But we've known about AIDS for 25 years now. So how did it get to this point?

Turning a Blind Eye

When AIDS was first identified, in the USA in 1981, evidence suggested that it was limited to certain high-risk groups, including gay men, haemophiliacs and IDUs. But when research in Central Africa in 1984 found that in the general population, AIDS affected men and women equally, it became clear that the threat was universal.

By 1986, epidemiologists understood that HIV/AIDS was a particular danger to the developing world and that a huge epidemic was already brewing in Central and East Africa. Later that year, the World Health Organization (WHO) acknowledged it was "a pandemic as mortal as any pandemic there has ever been" and promised to dedicate its "energy, commitment and creativity to the urgent, difficult and complex task of global AIDS prevention and control."

But 20 years on, campaigners are asking why more than 40 million people are now living with HIV. "HIV is very clever at spreading," says Ellman. "It leaves you looking healthy, feeling healthy, being fertile, being sexually active for ten years. During that time, you don't look any different from the rest of the population, but you're still spreading HIV." But the scientists knew that. More important have been the roles of stigma, denial, poverty, racism and politics.

Soon after the WHO's announcement, rich nations initiated education programmes and infection rates plummeted. But elsewhere governments dragged their feet or, worse still, buried their heads in the sand. "The scale of the problem was difficult to acknowledge," says Ellman. "Governments of poor nations had neither the funds nor the infrastructure required to deliver the appropriate response." Many hoped that a cure or vaccine would save them the trouble.

A Lack of Support for the Developing World

As Western nations began to realise that they had avoided a heterosexual epidemic, support for the developing world dried up. Research into treatments and vaccines was granted copious funding, but little went towards prevention. "The appropriate response would have been to implement massive prevention programmes in developing nations with every intervention available," says Jun Kim, director of the WHO's HIV/AIDS department. "But it was felt that interventions deployed in the First World were impossible in the Third World, so they were written off."

The first director of the WHO's special programme on HIV/AIDS, Jonathan Mann, was one of the few to show any real commitment. But political wrangling saw him resign in 1990, after which the programme's budget was cut. "In terms of HIV/AIDS, the WHO was really out of it from that point for the next ten years or so," says Kim.

In 1993, it was announced that preventing half of the 20 million new infections projected by 2000 would cost US$2.5billion a year—about 20 times the global AIDS budget at that time. Yet funding remained pitiful. The US government allocation for AIDS in developing nations remained at around US$70million for most of the 1990s. By 1997, the UK government was giving less than £40million a year.

According to Gregory Pappas, a senior policy advisor at the US Department of Health and Human Services during the 1990s, it was all about "demand management." The USA resisted paying for AIDS tests overseas at that time, he told the *Washington Post* in 2000. "The implications of a lot of people knowing they have HIV, instead of just dying of it, is [that] it creates demands on the development-assistance agencies."

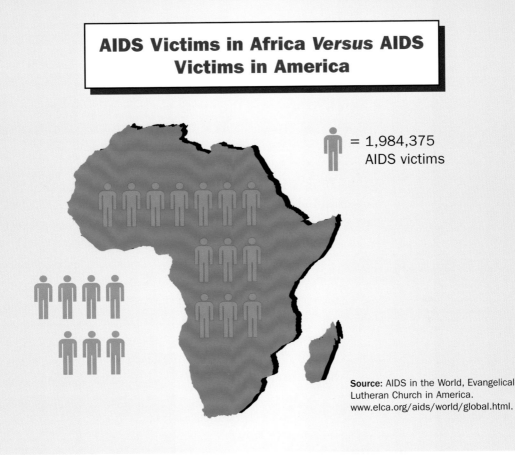

AIDS Victims in Africa *Versus* AIDS Victims in America

👤 = 1,984,375 AIDS victims

Source: AIDS in the World, Evangelical Lutheran Church in America. www.elca.org/aids/world/global.html.

As a slow-burn, chronic disaster, AIDS was never going to elicit funds, says Kim. "The things that attract money are immediate disasters such as the Asian tsunami or an earthquake, where you can save a child or prevent starvation. No one ever talked about saving lives or treating people living with HIV."

Treatment had been available to those who could afford it since the late 1980s. Yet it wasn't considered viable to provide it in the developing world. "This was partly because of the cost," says Ellman, "and partly because health systems weren't set up to deliver long-term care."

The Developed World Wakes Up

Then, suddenly, the USA decided to take HIV/AIDS seriously. Political will appeared to change overnight. In January 2000, the UN Security Council convened a special session to discuss HIV/AIDS—the first ever to consider a health issue—and the following year, all 189 members of the UN signed a declaration relating to treatment, prevention, protecting orphans, alleviating social and economic impacts, and research development.

In 2002, the Global Fund for AIDS, Malaria and TB was established to mobilise resources to fight these diseases in developing countries. The same year, George W. Bush announced that the President's Emergency Plan for AIDS Relief (PEPFAR) would commit an unprecedented US$15billion dollars between 2003 and 2008 to provide treatment to two million people, prevent seven million new infections and provide care to ten million people infected and affected by HIV/AIDS in the developing world. In 2003, the WHO launched its "3 by 5" initiative, which aimed to provide treatment to three million people—half of those most in need of ART in developing countries—by the end of 2005.

So is it all OK now?

Is There Any Hope?

Last June [2005], the WHO revealed that "3 by 5" wouldn't reach its target. It had only managed to increase the number of people on ART in developing countries from 400,000 to almost one million, only 15 per cent of those in need of treatment. Indeed, the estimated coverage in sub-Saharan Africa was only 11 per cent....

Ultimately, tackling HIV/AIDS is about more than just the pandemic itself, says Ellman. "Health has never attracted the money and attention it needs. That's why millions still die each year from preventable diseases such as measles and malaria. But HIV/AIDS is now a 'sexy' issue. We have to ensure that the commitment we have seen to HIV will lead to substantial improvements in health service delivery and in numbers of health workers across the board."

CHAPTER 2

Issues Concerning AIDS

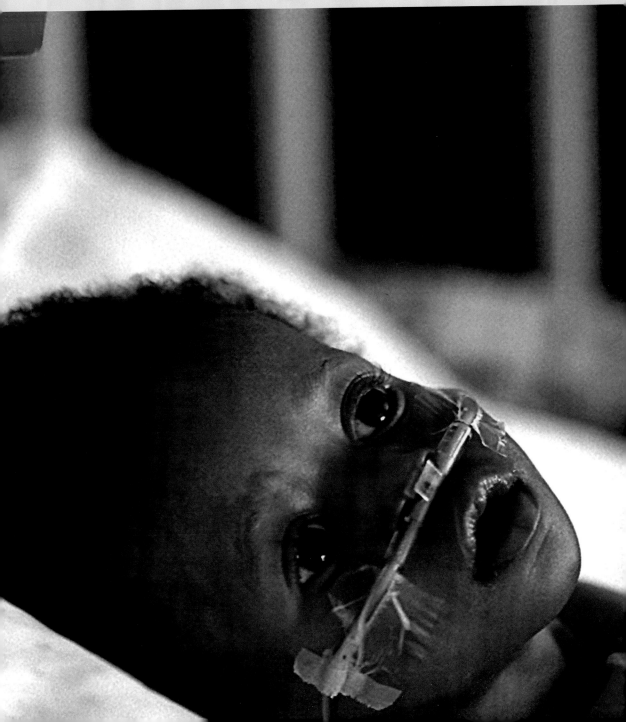

The Developed World Has a Moral Obligation to Fight AIDS in the Developing World

Diane Taylor

In this viewpoint, Diane Taylor argues that world leaders, and especially those of developed countries, are obliged to cooperate in the global and proactive fight to stop the AIDS pandemic. HIV infections continue to rise at alarming rates, Taylor states, and attempts to improve prevention, treatment, and care for HIV and AIDS have fallen far short of their proposed targets. Taylor explains that poverty is largely to blame because malnutrition and lack of drugs and education fuel the disease. The global community is aware of the possibilities for prevention, but leaders are not focusing on effective and adequate measures to combat the disease to the best of their abilities. Diane Taylor writes for the *Guardian* on topics including sex workers and women's rights.

Photo on previous page. A five-month-old victim of Africa's AIDS epidemic lies in a hospital bed in South Africa. (AP Images)

I n the 25 years since Aids has been with us, an awful lot of promises have been made by the world's most powerful people to tackle the epidemic. Government

SOURCE: Diane Taylor, "What More Can Be Done?" *The Guardian,* August 12, 2006. Reproduced by permission of the author.

leaders, the UN, the World Health Organisation and other bodies have pledged to pour money and other resources into taking on the scourge of the latter part of the 20th century in the hope that it won't blight too much of the 21st.

On the face of it they've failed miserably. Over the last 25 years almost 65 million people have become infected with HIV, 25 million have died of Aids-related illnesses and close to 40 million are living with the virus, the vast majority unaware of their status. [In 2005] alone there were 4.1 million new infections and 2.8 million people died. To date 15 million children have been orphaned by the virus and up to 400 million people are directly affected by the global pandemic.

A special session of the UN General Assembly (Ungass) in 2001 made a declaration of commitment on HIV and Aids. Leaders from 189 member states committed to comprehensive time-bound targets for the delivery of effective HIV prevention, treatment, care and support. They pledged to halt and reverse the global epidemic by 2015.

A series of targets were set for 2005 and overwhelmingly the 189 countries that made such fine promises have failed to deliver. By 2005, 90% of young people aged 15–24 were supposed to have the knowledge to correctly identify ways of preventing HIV transmission. In fact only 33% of males and 20% of females are equipped with this vital information. Eighty per cent of HIV positive pregnant women were supposed to be receiving prophylactic anti-retroviral treatment: in fact just 9% get these vital drugs. A 25% reduction in the number of young people becoming infected with the virus was pledged by 2005 yet there has only been a 4.1% reduction for 15- to 24-year-old females and only 1.6% for their male counterparts.

At the recent G8 [international forum representing eight national governments] meeting in St Petersburg leaders pledged to renew their commitment to fight Aids but endorsed no detailed plan and made no new funding commitments. Aids is now the world's leading cause of premature death among men and women aged 15–59. More than 95% of those living with HIV are in developing countries.

Concern is part of an alliance of six non-governmental organisations across Europe called Alliance 2015 which share a commitment to implementing both the Ungass declaration and the Millenium Development Goals: a series of health, development and poverty eradication targets set for 2015.

Breda Gahan, Concern's global HIV and Aids programme adviser says: "On almost all targets we have failed

Protestors in Entebbe, Uganda, hold up a banner as U.S. president George W. Bush's motorcade passes by. (**AP Images**)

miserably. If this was a school report we'd all be expelled. There are 14,000 new HIV infections every day and 8,000 people die needlessly from Aids-related illnesses every day—yet these deaths never make the headlines."

Despite the gloomy statistics a lot has been achieved at international, national and local levels to combat the virus, but because Aids is such a multi-headed hydra, unless every aspect is dealt with simultaneously and every condition which provides oxygen to the epidemic is crushed, it seems that the virus will continue to outwit all attempts to destroy it.

Poverty is the key driver for HIV. If people don't have enough to eat they get sicker than well-fed westerners who become infected. If they don't have jobs, particularly in rural areas, male members of households migrate to towns and cities to find work, breaking up family units in the process and often acquiring HIV from new partners or sex workers whom they meet when they leave home.

Providing anti-retroviral drugs (ARVs) for those who are infected without focusing equally on education to prevent the virus makes success very difficult. Further, poor education, gender inequality, lack of access to sexual and reproductive health services and rights violations allowing stigma and discrimination to develop, also help Aids to thrive.

Unlike diseases like malaria and tuberculosis, Aids is complicated by the fact that the majority of people acquire it either as a result of having unsafe sex or injecting drugs with unsterile needles. Both activities attract moral opprobrium from certain powerful quarters.

The USA, backed up by some Muslim states, wants to see sexual abstinence outside marriage used as a key tool to stem the epidemic. It opposes what other states such as the UK say is a morally neutral move of making condoms

> ## FAST FACT
>
> Every day at least sixteen thousand people are newly infected with HIV around the world.

available to everyone who has sex whatever are the circumstances of their sexual liaisons. The USA is also reluctant to embrace a proactive harm-reduction policy towards drug users which involves distributing free and plentiful supplies of sterile injecting equipment.

As UK secretary of state for international development Hilary Benn says, in setting out a clear demarcation line between the US and the UK positions, "difficult and uncomfortable truths" about the virus must be faced. "Abstinence is fine for those who are able to abstain, but human beings like to have sex and should not die because they do have sex," he says.

At the recent Ungass meeting, the more and less liberal states disagreed over the wording of updated pledges around sexual activity including commercial sex and drug use. Prudence Mabele, of the South African organisation Positive Women's Network, condemned leaders for not doing more to tackle the epidemic. "Our leaders have shown an utter lack of responsibility in standing up for the lives of 25 million HIV positive Africans," she said.

Reverend Njongonkulu Ndungane, the Anglican bishop of Cape Town, also criticised the lack of action from global leaders. "We call on the world's political leaders to rise up and meet the challenges that the pandemic presents and to set ambitious targets at a national level to guarantee universal access to treatment, care, support and prevention."

Non-governmental organisations were equally unhappy with the situation. Leonard Okello, head of HIV/Aids for ActionAid International, says: "The negotiation process was guided by trading political, economic and other interests of the big, powerful countries rather than the glaring facts and statistics of the global Aids crisis, 70% of which is in sub-Saharan Africa."

But despite the manifest failures on the global stage there are vast numbers of effective initiatives operating at a grassroots level all over the world, particularly in the

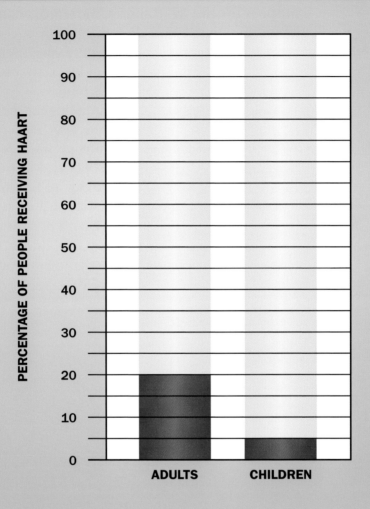

Percentage of HIV-Infected People in the Developing World Receiving HAART

PERCENTAGE OF PEOPLE RECEIVING HAART

ADULTS   CHILDREN

Source: Stephen Lewis, "When the Bottom Line Isn't Enough," *Communication World,* January–February 2007, p. 22.

most impoverished nations that are worst hit by the epidemic. Responses tailored to specific local circumstances are vital—what works well in rural Bangladesh won't necessarily translate into success in downtown Addis Ababa.

Civil society reports from more than 30 countries say that national governments, international partners and communities are failing to provide adequate care and support for the 15 million children orphaned by Aids while the stigma and discrimination encountered by people living with HIV is still pervasive. "A quarter of a century into the epidemic the global response stands at a crossroads," says a new UNAids report.

Breda Gahan remains optimistic that the right turning will be taken. "HIV is technically 100% preventable. We all have the capacity to protect ourselves if given the correct knowledge, power, respect and resources. We're all part of the problem and we can all be part of the solution. "We know what works, let's just do it a lot better and a lot faster so that we can have a positive impact. We need to believe that we can stop this epidemic. It is vital to sustain hope; otherwise we're going nowhere."

The Developed World Must Fight AIDS to Protect Global Security

Stephan Faris

The developed world should fight AIDS as a terrorist security threat as well as for humanitarian reasons, explains Stephan Faris in the following article. The United States, for example, is funding a good part of the military AIDS program in Uganda and other African countries. If military and police forces become too weakened by AIDS, governments in Africa and elsewhere will not be able to maintain civil order and put down subversive uprisings.

Journalist Stephan Faris has published articles on Africa, the Middle East, and China in major periodicals, including *Time, Fortune,* and the *Atlantic Monthly*.

In a dark-green shipping container outside a Ugandan military hospital, a visiting Tanzanian general and four of his colonels encircle a desk. On the desk sits a

SOURCE: Stephan Faris, "Containment Strategy: Iran. North Korea. Uganda? Why the Pentagon Ranks Africa's AIDS Epidemic as a Leading Security Threat," *The Atlantic Monthly*, vol. 298, December 2006, pp. 34–35. Copyright © 2006 by The Atlantic Monthly Group. All rights reserved. Reproduced by permission.

green plastic paper tray. And from the tray rises a polished wooden dildo [a penis-shaped object]. "This weapon," a Ugandan warrant officer tells them, "I'm sorry for exposing it to you. This is one of the weapons we have used in fighting HIV and AIDS."

In the Ugandan military's program for AIDS prevention and treatment, the dildo is used to demonstrate condom use. It is part of the first line of defense in a larger conflict that very much involves American forces: the fight to prevent countries from collapsing into failed states that can foment armed conflict, chaos, and terrorism beyond their borders. In fact, the United States Department of Defense funds a good part of the Ugandan military's AIDS program. It trains doctors and clinicians, helps support AIDS orphans, and stocks labs with instruments and supplies. And it has donated thirteen prefabricated HIV-testing labs and AIDS-counseling centers, including the one in which the officers were sitting on a summer afternoon out at the Bombo Barracks, about an hour's drive from Kampala.

The impact of AIDS on Africa's health and well-being is a matter of grim statistical record. By 2010, USAID [the U.S. Agency for International Development] estimates, the epidemic will have cut the life expectancy in Botswana to twenty-seven years from what would have been at least seventy years. Some countries expect to lose half a generation. "When you have countries where you have 40 percent of the adult population affected, where teachers are disproportionately infected, where we're creating a generation of orphans, you can see the stress on the social fabric," says Ambassador Mark R. Dybul, the U.S. global AIDS coordinator.

But what was once seen as a humanitarian catastrophe is viewed increasingly as a security threat—an important reason behind the $15 billion Emergency Plan

FAST FACT

In 2000 President Bill Clinton added AIDS to a list of national security threats, which included terrorism and nuclear weapons.

for AIDS Relief that President [George W.] Bush announced in January 2003. A study of 112 countries by Susan Peterson, a political scientist at the College of William and Mary, and Stephen Shellman, a political scientist at the University of Georgia, found that countries with severe AIDS epidemics had correspondingly high levels of human-rights abuse and civil conflict. "Does

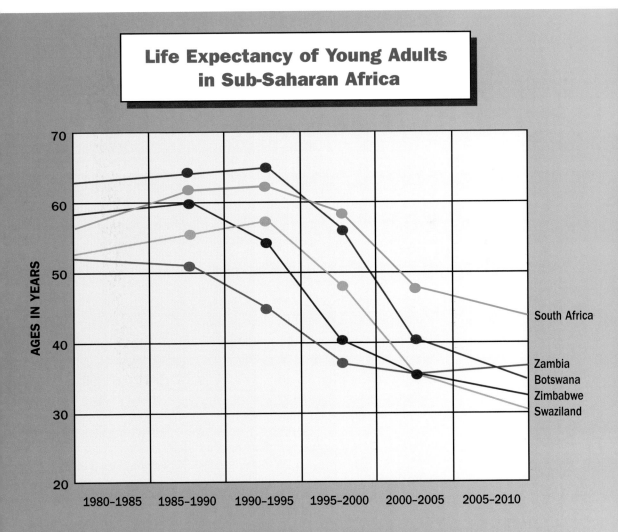

Life Expectancy of Young Adults in Sub-Saharan Africa

Life expectancy at birth in selected countries most affected by HIV/AIDS, 1980–1985 through 2006–2010.

Source: Charlie Furniss, "AIDS Crisis: 25 Years On," *Geographical*, January 2006, p. 47.

AIDS make war or civil strife more likely?" asks Peterson. "The answer is yes."

Even in countries that don't collapse, AIDS deaths can threaten security in the form of AIDS orphans, who are desperate, disenfranchised, vulnerable to radicalization, and projected to reach 25 million worldwide by 2010. "Where do you think the breeding ground for terrorism will be?" asks General Charles Wald, the former operational head of European Command, which also oversees U.S. military operations in most of Africa. At a recent conference, Wald listed the biggest threats to U.S. security. After terrorism and weapons of mass destruction came AIDS.

The Pentagon's Concerns

High on the list of the Pentagon's concerns about AIDS is its impact on African militaries; for many, it has become the biggest killer. Young, often far from home, and with cash in their pockets, soldiers who must fight under fire cultivate a sense of invulnerability that can kill them when they come back to the barracks. The epidemic accounts for seven out of ten military deaths in South Africa and kills more Ugandan soldiers than any other cause, including a brutal twenty-year insurgency and two wars in Congo. AIDS deaths have reduced Malawi's forces by 40 percent. Mozambique can't train police officers fast enough to replace those dying of the disease. "As we fight the enemy, the HIV is also fighting us," John Amosa, a forty-five-year-old AIDS-afflicted Ugandan sergeant, told me. "We have two front lines."

Uganda kicked off the fight that became a model for AIDS prevention in 1986, after President Yoweri Museveni sent sixty of his top officers for training in Cuba, where eighteen tested positive for HIV. At a conference later that year, Fidel Castro took the Ugandan president aside. "He said, 'You've got a big problem on your hands,'" recalled Sam Kibende, a deputy director of Uganda's na-

Protestors rally in Cape Town, South Africa, to demand stronger action to combat the AIDS epidemic in that country. Those dressed in red are HIV-positive. (**AP Images**)

tional AIDS research center. "That's when the president woke up and realized his fighting force was going to be decimated." With national infection rates leveling off somewhere between 6 and 7 percent after peaking at 15 percent in the early 1990s, the Ugandan army plans to hold every officer responsible for AIDS education.

"Behavior change needs sustained fire," says Dr. Stephen Kusasira, who runs the Ugandan military's anti-AIDS efforts. "We want it to be a command problem. It should only become a medical situation when they are sick."

AIDS Hinders Security in Africa

Unfortunately, AIDS hampers the ability of Uganda and other African nations to maintain not only their own security but also that of their neighbors. Asked to send troops to the troubled Darfur region of Sudan, South Africa couldn't field a complete battalion of uninfected troops; an estimated 17 to 23 percent of its military is HIV-positive, and tests in 2004 on two battalions found infection rates as high as 80 percent. "They had to kludge together units to get enough healthy troops to send," says Wald, who retired from his post at European Command in July [2006]. Because African Union members contribute 37 percent of all United Nations peacekeepers, the shortage of healthy manpower has rippled out through the world's hot spots and is of growing concern to the United States, which leaves peacekeeping duties mostly to other nations. "AIDS is a readiness issue," says Richard Shaffer, a retired Navy commander who runs the Defense Department's HIV/AIDS Prevention Program. "It's not just having your weapon. It's not just knowing how to use it. It's being healthy enough to use it."

Perhaps the only thing worse than having few peacekeepers ready to send is the risk to those who actually go. Eighty-one percent of UN peacekeepers are on missions in Africa, home to 60 percent of the world's people living with AIDS. A 1999 study by the head of Nigeria's medical corps found that the longer Nigeria's soldiers were deployed as peacekeepers in Sierra Leone, the greater their chance of contracting HIV. Infection rates increased from 7 percent after one year abroad to 10 percent after two years, and to more than 15 percent after three years.

It's not hard to see why. During a short stay in the Congolese city of Goma last year, I was shown a dozen or so children allegedly fathered by soldiers from the UN mission, including two light-skinned boys whose fathers were said to be Moroccan. One visitor to Bunia, where the fighting is most brutal, said that she had seen women stripping in the headlights of vehicles of soldiers on night patrol. "The United Nations has helped me a lot," Bibishe, a twenty-five-year-old prostitute, told me. "They bought me the mattress I'm sleeping on. They bought me clothes." In the courtyard of her brothel waited a drunken South African sergeant. It was about ten o'clock in the morning.

Since its beginnings in 1981, AIDS has infected about 65 million people worldwide, and killed more than 25 million of them. Yet in parts of Africa, the first waves of death are just beginning. Andrew Price-Smith, a political scientist at Colorado College, cites Zimbabwe, where the epidemic accelerated a general slide into chaos, as a warning of what might happen in other countries. "We've already peaked in terms of infections," says Price-Smith. "Now we're starting to see the mortalities crest. The subsequent wave will be the wave of economic and political disruption that follows." Nigeria is another focus of concern, not so much because of its infection rate (which, at between 4 and 6 percent, is relatively low) but because of its general instability and its importance as an oil supplier. "When AIDS affects a large portion of a population, that creates instability," said General William "Kip" Ward, who took over Wald's position. "That instability can lead to conditions that are right for terrorist exploitation as they seek to recruit new followers." While the security threat that AIDS poses is for now largely confined to Africa and Southeast Asia, stirrings of epidemics in Russia and India (which happens to be the third-biggest contributor of UN peacekeepers) are, given their size, strength, and strategic importance, more worrisome still.

Thinking Prevention

As the U.S. military pivots to confront these risks, it's starting to have to think preventively. The Navy—whose Naval Health Research Center is a leader in military research on behavioral issues—oversees and funds prevention and treatment programs in sixty-seven countries. In Vietnam, U.S. forces teach AIDS prevention to the army they once fought. In Ukraine, they're setting up testing and counseling centers. In India, they're providing clinical training and lab support. "We can't just sit back and wait until the crisis is fully blown and treat every problem like it's the nail and we're the hammer," says Wald.

The spectacular rollout of antiretroviral medication may be stopping the gap across Africa, but treatment programs will remain hostage to donor funding and vulnerable to viral resistance to drugs. Future military missions may increasingly be like the AIDS-vaccine research project in western Kenya, where the Walter Reed Army Institute of Research helps care for 2.5 million civilians on the tea plantations around the city of Kericho and in the neighboring Southern Rift Valley. The Army provides 6,500 patients with antiretroviral drugs and supports a youth center along with church-based counseling and in-home care. It has renovated the district hospital and brought in more staff and doctors. To teach AIDS sufferers the basics of nutrition and feed them in the meantime, Walter Reed has even planted a model farm, complete with rows of maize and grazing areas for three cows and their calves. "The main mission is [vaccine] development for the American war fighter," says Colonel Samuel Martin, commander of Walter Reed in Kenya. "This just helps us put a more human dimension to our operations." In the leafy hills around Kericho, the Army is hoping to keep Americans safe by helping Africans to stay alive.

Herpes and Poverty Are Responsible for the AIDS Epidemic in Africa

Emily Oster

In the following article, economist Emily Oster argues that sexual practices in Africa are not responsible for the AIDS epidemic. Instead, she blames the prevalence of genital herpes, which causes sores that admit the HIV virus into the bloodstream, and universal poverty, which lowers life expectancy to the point that Africans do not protect themselves from a disease that may kill them in ten years.

Emily Oster received her PhD in economics at Harvard and is currently a Becker Fellow at the University of Chicago.

When I began studying the HIV epidemic in Africa a few years ago, there were few other economists working on the topic and almost none on the specific issues that interested me. It's not that the questions I wanted to answer weren't being asked. They were. But they were being asked by anthropologists, sociologists, and public-health officials.

That's an important distinction. These disciplines believe that cultural differences—differences in how entire groups of people think and act—account for broader social and regional trends. AIDS became a disaster in Africa, the thinking goes, because Africans didn't know how to deal with it.

Economists like me don't trust that argument. We assume everyone is fundamentally alike; we believe circumstances, not culture, drive people's decisions, including decisions about sex and disease.

I've studied the epidemic from that perspective. I'm one of the few people who have done so. And I've learned that a lot of what we've been told about it is wrong. Below are three things the world needs to know about AIDS in Africa.

FAST FACT

Up to 11 percent of people in Africa have untreated sexually transmitted infections, which can cause open sores and can greatly increase the transmission of HIV.

1) It's the Wrong Disease to Attack

Approximately 6 percent of adults in sub-Saharan Africa are infected with HIV; in the United States, the number is around 0.8 percent. Very often, this disparity is attributed to differences in sexual behavior—in the number of sexual partners, the types of sexual activities, and so on. But these differences cannot, in fact, be seen in the data on sexual behavior. So what actually accounts for the gulf in infection rates?

According to my research, the major difference lies in transmission rates of the virus. For a given unprotected sexual relationship with an HIV-infected person, Africans are between four and five times more likely than Americans to become infected with HIV themselves. This stark fact accounts for virtually all of the difference in population-wide HIV rates in the two regions.

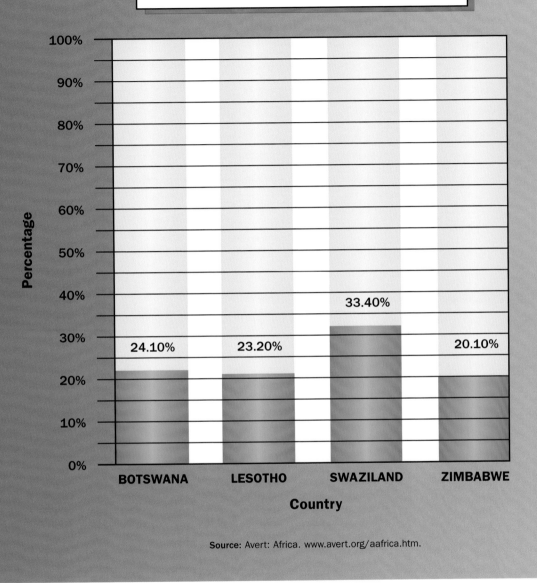

Percentage of HIV-Infected Individuals in African Countries

Source: Avert: Africa. www.avert.org/aafrica.htm.

There is more than one reason why HIV spreads more easily in Africa than America, but the most important one seems to be related to the prevalence of other sexually transmitted infections. Estimates suggest that around 11 percent of individuals in Africa have untreated bacterial sexually transmitted infections at any given time and close to half have the herpes virus. Because many of these infections cause open sores on the genitals, transmission of the HIV virus is much more efficient.

So what do we learn from this? First, the fact that Africa is so heavily affected by HIV has very little to do with differences in sexual behavior and very much to do with differences in circumstances. Second, and perhaps more important, there is potential for significant reductions in HIV transmission in Africa through the treatment of other sexually transmitted diseases. Such an

Refugees wait for aid at a Doctors Without Borders station in Ndele, Angola. Some argue that deep and widespread poverty in Africa is a major reason for the AIDS epidemic there. (AP Images)

approach would cost around $3.50 per year per life saved. Treating AIDS itself costs around $300 per year. There are reasons to provide AIDS treatment in Africa, but cost-effectiveness is not one of them.

2) It Won't Disappear Until Poverty Does

In the United States, the discovery of the HIV epidemic led to dramatic changes in sexual behavior. In Africa, it didn't. Yet in both places, encouraging safe sexual behavior has long been standard practice. Why haven't the lessons caught on in Africa?

The key is to think about why we expect people to change their behavior in response to HIV—namely because, in a world with HIV, sex carries a larger risk of death than it does in a world without HIV. But how much people care about dying from AIDS ten years from now depends on how many years they expect to live today and how enjoyable they expect those future years to be.

My studies show that while there have been very limited changes in sexual behavior in Africa on average, Africans who are richer or who live in areas with higher life expectancies have changed their behavior more. And men in Africa have responded in almost exactly the same way to their relative "life forecasts" as gay men in the United States did in the 1980s. To put it bluntly, if income and life expectancy in Africa were the same as they are in the United States, we would see the same change in sexual behavior—and the AIDS epidemic would begin to slow.

3) There Is Less of It than We Thought —but It's Spreading as Fast as Ever

According to the UN, the HIV rates in Botswana and Zimbabwe are around 30 percent, and it's more than 10 percent in many other countries. These estimates are relied on by policymakers, researchers, and the popular press. Yet many people who study the AIDS epidemic believe that the numbers are inflated.

The reason is quite simple: bias in who is tested. The UN's estimates are not based on diagnoses of whole populations or even a random sample. They are based on tests of pregnant women at prenatal clinics. And in Africa, sexually active women of child-bearing age have the highest rates of HIV infection.

To eliminate the bias, I took a new approach to estimating the HIV infection rate: I inferred it from mortality data. The idea is simple: In a world without HIV, we have some expectation of what the death rate will be. In a world with HIV, we observe the actual death rate to be higher. The difference between the two gives an estimate of the number of people who have died from AIDS, and we can use that figure to estimate the prevalence of HIV in the population.

My work suggests that the HIV rates reported by the UN are about three times too high. Which sounds like good news—but isn't. The overall number of HIV-positive people may be lower than we thought, but my study, which estimated changes in the infection rate over time, also drew a second, chilling conclusion: In Africa, HIV is spreading as quickly as ever.

Cultural Traditions of Sexual Behavior Are Responsible for the AIDS Epidemic in Africa

Mike Crawley

In the following article, author Mike Crawley discusses how HIV prevention in Africa is proving difficult because of cultural values regarding sexual behavior among African men and women. He argues that changing the behavior of the African people is a challenge. The men are used to traditions such as male dominance, a reluctance to talk openly about sex, and an acceptance of polygamy that allows husbands to have multiple sexual partners. Women, on the other hand, do not have the economic or social power to demand safe sex, such as expecting the use of condoms. Mike Crawley is a correspondent for the *Christian Science Monitor*.

Messages about how to prevent HIV have been spread to all corners of Africa. AIDS education programs take place in schools in Kenya, churches in Uganda, workplaces in Botswana, and even bus stations here in Ghana. Yet the stark numbers in a

SOURCE: Mike Crawley, "Why AIDS Keeps Spreading in Africa," *Christian Science Monitor*, December 1, 2004. Reproduced by permission of the author.

new United Nations report suggests these efforts are failing to persuade millions of Africans to change their sexual behavior.

The UN AIDS Epidemic Update 2004, launched to mark Wednesday's World AIDS Day, estimates about 5 million people over the past year contracted the virus that causes AIDS, and predicts another 5 million will do the same next year. Most of those people—3.1 million, or 63 percent—are here in Africa.

Translating Awareness to Behavior Change Proves Difficult

Awareness levels around the world are higher than they've ever been, but so is the pace at which the virus spread, according to the report. The real hurdle, say observers, is translating awareness into behavior change, and the effort often runs up against longstanding and strongly held cultural values.

"If the same market researchers who are selling Coke were charged with selling safer sex, they'd probably have thrown up their hands by now because it's a much more complicated thing," says Neill McKee, coauthor of the book *Strategic Communication in the HIV/AIDS Epidemic.*

Here in sub-Saharan Africa some of those cultural stumbling blocks include male dominance, a reluctance to talk openly about sex, and a tradition of polygamy that today manifests itself in tacit acceptance of married men having multiple sexual partners. African men who have become disempowered through a history of colonialism, racism, and poor economic prospects are unwilling to give up the power they hold over women, says Suzanne Leclerc-Madlala, head of anthropology at South Africa's University of KwaZulu-Natal.

"I don't think we're putting enough emphasis on changing men's behavior," says Ms. Leclerc-Madlala. She says a key solution is for male African leaders—whether

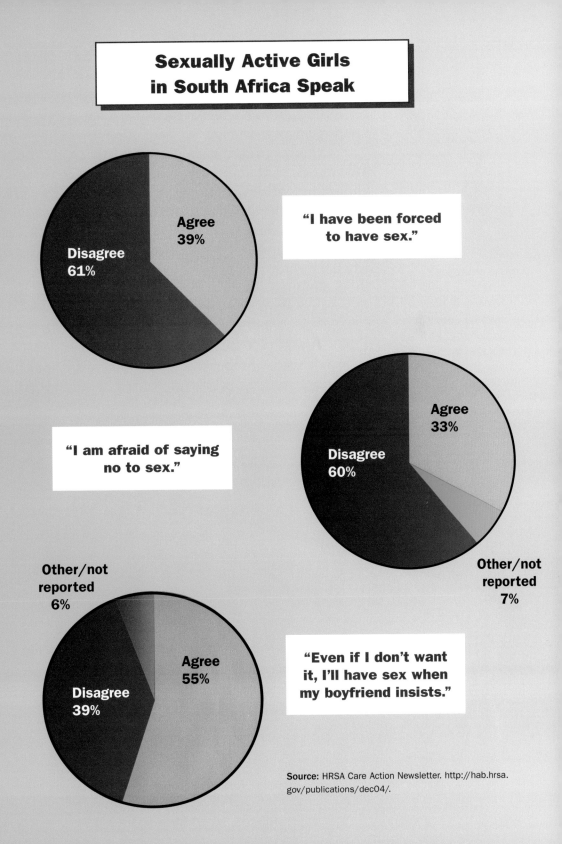

Sexually Active Girls in South Africa Speak

Agree 39%

Disagree 61%

"I have been forced to have sex."

"I am afraid of saying no to sex."

Agree 33%

Disagree 60%

Other/not reported 7%

Other/not reported 6%

Agree 55%

Disagree 39%

"Even if I don't want it, I'll have sex when my boyfriend insists."

Source: HRSA Care Action Newsletter. http://hab.hrsa. gov/publications/dec04/.

politicians, sports figures, or traditional rulers—to take a stand, admit publicly that men's behavior is a problem, and urge men to change.

"The prevention strategies are missing the point. Women do not have the economic power or social choices over their lives to put the information into practice," said Kathleen Cravero, deputy executive director of the UN joint program on AIDS, during a press conference in London last week. "We tell women to abstain when they have no right. We tell them to be faithful when they cannot ask their partners to be faithful. We tell them to use a condom when they have no power to do so."

The "ABC" Principles

Research into whether young people in sub-Saharan Africa are putting into practice the so-called "ABC"

A microbicide gel applicator, a form of HIV prevention women can control, is demonstrated at a hospital in Soweto, South Africa.
(AP Images)

principles—abstain, be faithful, or use a condom—shows, at best, mixed results. The country often singled out as Africa's biggest AIDS-prevention success story is Uganda, where HIV infection rates have dropped to 4.1 percent from a peak of 13 percent in the early 1990s. Research has attributed some of this decline to programs that succeeded in persuading young people to delay their first sexual experiences and to increase condom use. But elsewhere in Africa, condom use is increasing only in some countries, and the proportion of men and women engaging in extramarital sex is not declining.

The new UN report points to "gradual, modest declines" in HIV prevalence in some urban areas of Kenya and Ethiopia but cautions: "It is much too early to claim that these recent declines herald a definitive reversal in these countries' epidemics."

Simply knowing how HIV is transmitted wasn't enough for Julius Amoako, a Ghanaian man who tested positive for the virus two years ago. He believes he caught it from his girlfriend. "I thought HIV was a thing for people who are prostitutes or gay, not someone like me," he says.

"People, especially the youth, don't think the disease is there among them," says Samuel Benefour, senior program officer with Family Health International, a US-based development agency. Mr. Benefour runs a behavior-change communication program in the Manya Krobo and Yilo Krobo districts, about 50 miles north of the Ghanaian capital, Accra.

HIV-Prevention Efforts

A significant chunk of on-the-ground HIV education worldwide is done by volunteers like Emmanuel Awaitey. Mr. Awaitey goes door-to-door here in Abanse, a densely populated strip of a town stretched out along the main road through Manya Krobo district. On a recent day, he approaches a courtyard where two young women are preparing lunch and doing laundry and asks them what they know about HIV. He spends half an hour talking with the women. It's a time-consuming process, but it's face-to-face work like this that Benefour wants to see more of.

Some HIV-prevention efforts are turning more attention to giving people life skills that empower them to say no to unsafe sex. Until recently, the main activities of the Ghana Social Marketing Foundation (GSMF) have been selling condoms and spreading the safer-sex message through mass media. It has plastered more than 300,000 AIDS awareness bumper stickers on the country's taxis and *tro-tros*, the mini-buses that provide much of the urban and long-distance transport here.

Targeting the country's transport hubs as a vector for the spread of HIV led the foundation to work with the female hawkers who scrape out a living selling food and drink at the *tro-tro* stations. These women are often financially dependent on men, making it hard for them to refuse sex, especially when it comes with the promise of some cash.

"We realized a way to control (the spread of HIV) is to increase the empowerment of women," says Rudi Lokko, GSMF chief of operations. Instead of simply teaching the hawkers about HIV prevention, GSMF has started training them in business skills and helping them access microcredit.

FAST FACT

With an infection rate of 55 percent, women represent the majority of HIV infections in sub-Saharan Africa.

Antiretroviral Drugs (ARVs) Will Curb the African AIDS Epidemic

Peter Gyves

In sub-Saharan Africa, women and children suffer disproportionately from HIV/AIDS. Seventy-five percent of women with HIV/AIDS live in sub-Saharan Africa and account for 60 percent of adults worldwide living with the disease, although sub-Saharan Africa accounts for only 10 percent of the world's population. The region accounts for 90 percent of the world's HIV-infected children. In five optimistic steps, Peter Gyves defines what the developed world should do about the situation.

Peter Gyves is a pediatrician whose practice includes Central America and sub-Saharan Africa, where he has treated HIV/AIDS in children.

In sub-Saharan Africa, where antiretroviral therapy has increased more than eightfold since the end of 2003, great strides are being made in treating patients with

SOURCE: Peter Gyves, "A Tale of Two Worlds: Children with H.I.V./AIDS," *America*, vol. 195, November 2006, p. 16. Copyright © 2006 America Press. All rights reserved. Reproduced by permission of America Press. For subscription information, visit www.america magazine.org.

H.I.V./AIDS. Those in the know, like participants in the 16th International AIDS Conference held last April [2005] in Toronto, Canada, express great optimism about treating the disease in the developing world. The United Nations' Global Fund, the U.S. president's Emergency Plan for AIDS Relief and the Bill and Melinda Gates Foundation have directed funds to this part of the world and made rapid progress possible. Although such optimism is largely justified, much work remains to be done, especially in preventing and treating H.I.V./AIDS in children.

Visiting African Hospitals

Over the past three years, I have visited Kenya, Chad, South Africa and Zambia to understand better the changes taking place in the care of people infected by H.I.V. What I have learned is that progress in preventing and treating the disease in children lags far behind the advances made in treating adults, and that among adults men fare significantly better than women.

During a recent visit to the university teaching hospital in Lusaka, the capital of Zambia, I met with staff physicians responsible for the care of children admitted with a variety of illnesses, including H.I.V./AIDS. I accompanied the chief pediatrician as she examined a child—H.I.V. positive, with severe anemia and malnutrition—and noticed another physician across the ward applying oxygen to an infant. By the time we approached this baby and her mother, the examining physician had just removed the oxygen from the child's face. The mother began to cry as a nurse wrapped the infant in a sheet and carried her away; her tiny daughter had died before much could be done to help her. The mother had brought her, in severe respiratory distress, to the hospital from an outlying clinic, because it had been unable to care for her baby. The examining physician told us that the infant was about 4 months old and appeared wasted. He thought it possible, even likely, that both the infant and her mother were

H.I.V. positive and that the baby had died from an untreated AIDS-related pneumonia. Neither the mother's nor the infant's H.I.V. status was known.

This sad but familiar scenario, one I had seen several times before in visits to sub-Saharan Africa, was an unpleasant reminder that despite increased access to antiretroviral therapy in this part of the world, childhood death is frequently H.I.V.-related.

AIDS Devastation in Sub-Saharan Africa

The magnitude of the problem is striking. Since AIDS was first recognized in 1981, H.I.V. has infected 65 million people and killed 25 million of them. Today 38.6 million people live with H.I.V. Of these, 24.5 million—64 percent of the world's total—are in sub-Saharan Africa, an area that contains only 10 percent of the world's population. Women and children suffer disproportionately. For example, 75 percent of all women with H.I.V. live in sub-Saharan Africa; they account for almost 60 percent of the adults living with the disease there. Despite this, only 6 percent of pregnant women in sub-Saharan Africa are offered treatment to prevent mother-to-child transmission of the virus. It is not surprising then that some 2 million children in the region live with H.I.V., which is almost 90 percent of the world's H.I.V.-infected children. Still, only 7 percent of the people receiving antiretroviral therapy in sub-Saharan Africa are children. Among the enormous consequences of H.I.V. infection in the region are an estimated 12 million orphans.

Mother-to-Child Transmission

The number of children with H.I.V. worldwide is directly linked to the number of pregnant women with the disease, and mother-to-child transmission is the most common way that children become infected. In the United States, the near universal access of pregnant women to a combination of antiretroviral therapy and intensive

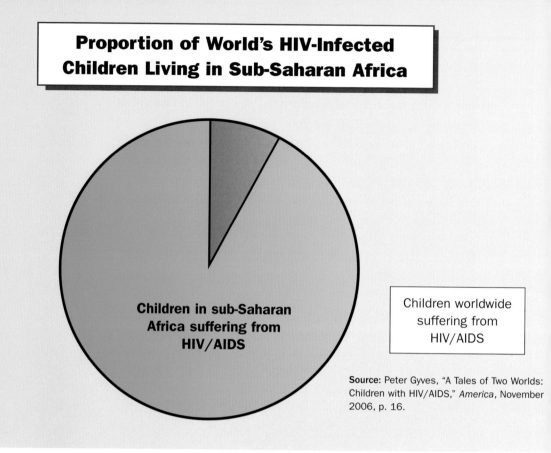

Proportion of World's HIV-Infected Children Living in Sub-Saharan Africa

Children in sub-Saharan Africa suffering from HIV/AIDS

Children worldwide suffering from HIV/AIDS

Source: Peter Gyves, "A Tales of Two Worlds: Children with HIV/AIDS," *America*, November 2006, p. 16.

surveillance of those treated has reduced the transmission rate to approximately 1 percent (down from 25 percent before antiretroviral therapy was provided).

What a contrast to the situation in sub-Saharan Africa, where access to such preventive programs is limited. Access varies from country to country and within countries and reflects the financial resources of a country, access to treatment centers of any kind, problems in identifying H.I.V.-positive pregnant women and varying levels of training among the health personnel who deliver and monitor the programs. Moreover, mother-to-child prevention programs in sub-Saharan Africa usually offer pregnant women a single dose of antiretroviral therapy at the onset of labor and one dose to the newborn within the first 72 hours of life. This strategy has decreased the mother-to-child transmission of H.I.V.

from approximately 25 percent to 11 percent. The simplified, shorter course of antiretroviral therapy is related to cost and the inherent difficulties in monitoring those receiving treatment.

Breast-feeding by H.I.V.-positive women is problematic. It increases the risk of transmitting the virus to babies by 5 to 15 percent over their first two years of life. Consequently, in sub-Saharan Africa the overall risk that mothers who have not received preventive treatment will transmit the virus to their newborns reaches 30 to 40 percent. Even the women benefitting from prevention therapy still incur a risk of some 15 to 25 percent. Despite the additional risk, the practice of breast feeding continues to be encouraged, because it protects against bacterial intestinal infections and ultimately carries less risk of death to H.I.V.-positive infants than do the alternatives: using formulas and solid foods during the early months of life.

> **FAST FACT**
>
> The price of AIDS treatment for a child may cost more than six times that to treat an adult: thirteen hundred dollars compared with two hundred dollars.

A worldwide view of H.I.V. infection in children sees two very different worlds. While few infants with H.I.V. are currently being born in the United States, the number of infected infants born in sub-Saharan Africa remains alarmingly high. The nearly universal availability of programs to prevent mother-to-child transmission in the United States is further enhanced by physicians' ability to identify H.I.V.-positive infants quickly and to offer high-tech treatment. Caregivers can quantify the amount of H.I.V. in the body, monitor drug levels to ensure a therapeutic effect, determine whether the virus is resistant to individual antiretroviral drugs and provide access to newer classes of antiretrovirals and antibiotics.

In sub-Saharan Africa, by contrast, identifying H.I.V. in infants is mostly limited to antibody testing, which often produces false positive results during the first 18 months of life because of interference from maternal antibodies. While treatment in this setting usually consists of a variation of the combination antiretroviral drugs used in the United States, surveillance remains a major obstacle. Issues range from the need to refrigerate some antiretroviral drugs to the prohibitive costs of high-tech laboratory testing and medicines.

Attainable Goals

U.S. standards for the prevention and treatment of children with H.I.V. are unrealistic for sub-Saharan Africa at the present time. Still, several attainable goals would significantly lower the prevalence of H.I.V. in children there and increase the survival time of children already infected. Here are some of them:

1. Increase dramatically the percentage of pregnant women enrolled in programs to prevent mother-to-child transmission (the current level is only 6 percent). These programs must also move toward the combination drug therapy and surveillance system offered in the United States.

2. Make the prevention and treatment of all women with H.I.V. a high priority.

3. Improve the general health care of H.I.V.-infected children, especially those under the age of 2. Improvement would include timely immunization against common childhood diseases and reducing the prevalence of malnutrition, tuberculosis and the most common causes of child deaths in the developing world —malaria and intestinal and respiratory diseases.

4. Provide care and monitoring for children who need combination antiretroviral therapy. That would entail a commitment to increase significantly the percentage of children receiving the therapy (from the current level of 7 percent) and a shift toward more high-tech treatment.

A mother holds up her six-month-old baby in the home for the destitute where she lives in Bulawayo, Zimbabwe. She transmitted HIV to the child during pregnancy, something that antiretroviral drugs might have prevented. **(AP Images)**

5. Encourage governments of the developed and developing worlds to respond to the plight of children with H.I.V. in sub-Saharan Africa, allocating more H.I.V. funding for children and pregnant women.

Without progress in these areas, large numbers of children in sub-Saharan Africa will continue to be born with H.I.V. and to die long before their time. The current contrast demonstrates that the story of children with H.I.V./AIDS is a tale of two very different worlds. The achievement of the developed world in preventing and treating children with H.I.V. is arguably the greatest success story to date in the struggle to control AIDS, yet it stands as a tragedy alongside the number of children who are dying of the same disease in the developing world.

Drug Companies Are Responsible for a Lack of AIDS Treatment in the Developing World

Daniel Pepper

According to author Daniel Pepper, Western drug companies are waging a battle against generic drug manufacturers in the developing world. Pepper claims that these companies are trying to stop the production of inexpensive antiretroviral drugs (ARVs) that HIV/AIDS sufferers in the developing world can afford.

Daniel Pepper is a writer and photojournalist focusing on human rights and social justice issues. His articles and photographs have appeared in *Time*, *Newsweek*, *Fortune*, and the *New York Times Magazine*.

O n the top floor of a drab apartment building on the edge of New Delhi, Ram Meher, 35, is taking his AIDS medicine, as he has every day for the past three years. Meher is a struggling wheat and sugarcane farmer who sold one of his three acres in 2003 for money to buy antiretroviral pills, which cost $125 a month. Before that he was swindled out of $477 by a traditional healer claiming to have a cure for the virus. Last year Meher switched to a generic version of the pills, which cost only $36 a month. "I wouldn't know what to do but pray to God," says Meher when asked what he would do if the low-cost drug, Duovir, manufactured by Indian generics company Cipla, weren't available. "There is no alternative after this."

Meher is one of an estimated 5.7 million Indians who make up the world's largest HIV-infected population. Access to generic versions of brand-name drugs means an extra ten to 15 years of life for many Indians, a quarter of whom live on less than $1 a day. But with battles now being waged over patents for the drugs that Indian pharmaceutical companies copy, the question on many

Protestors march on the U.S. Embassy in Pretoria, South Africa, accusing drug companies of seeking profits rather than saving lives. (**AP Images**)

people's minds is how much longer cheap generics will be available.

Cipla's Duovir is an antiretroviral combination drug widely used in AIDS-treatment programs throughout Latin America and Africa. It also has the dubious distinction of being the first generic anti-AIDS drug to come under attack by a Western pharmaceutical company, GlaxoSmithKline, which filed a patent application in India in 1997 for its drug Combivir, on which Duovir is based. Because the two antiretrovirals in Combivir were invented before 1995, when India signed the international intellectual-property-rights agreement known as TRIPS, they are not patentable in India. But Glaxo argues that the science behind combining the two drugs in Combivir—using the binding agent sodium dioxide, a form of sand—is more recent and warrants a 20-year patent.

Combivir is just the tip of the iceberg: India's patent offices are set to examine the patents for thousands of life-saving drugs in the coming months as it tries to bring its laws and practices in line with World Trade Organization regulations. Glaxo says the patent will have no impact on the price or availability of Combivir and that generic manufacturers will be able to apply for licenses and pay nominal royalties.

But for Leena Menghaney, who heads the campaign for access to essential medicines in New Delhi for Doctors Without Borders, that's irrelevant. "A combination of two drugs in one pill is not considered an invention under Indian patent law," says Menghaney, whose organization uses generic versions of Combivir in most of its AIDS-treatment programs around the world. "This is a clear case of trivial patenting by Glaxo." Cipla CEO Yussuf Hamied agrees. "There is no chance the Combivir

FAST FACT

Brazil began producing generic drugs to treat HIV and AIDS in 1998 and has since reduced the cost of treatment by 70 to 98 percent.

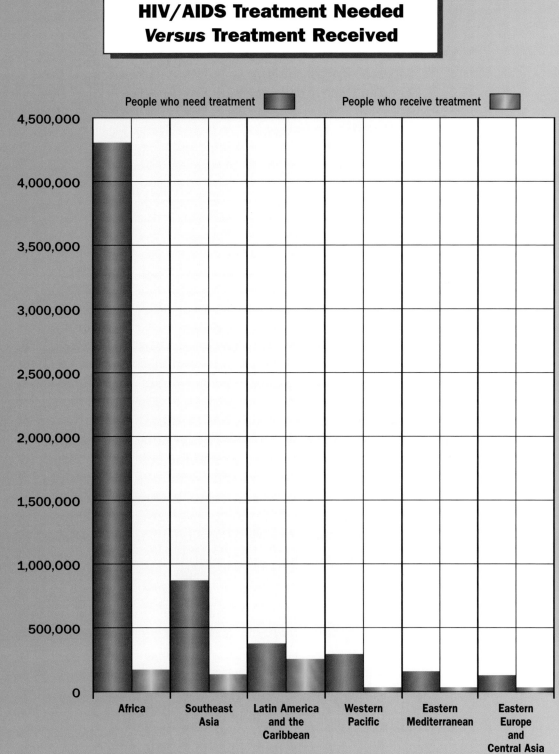

HIV/AIDS Treatment Needed *Versus* Treatment Received

People who need treatment ▮   People who receive treatment ▮

NUMBER OF PEOPLE

4,500,000
4,000,000
3,500,000
3,000,000
2,500,000
2,000,000
1,500,000
1,000,000
500,000
0

Africa   Southeast Asia   Latin America and the Caribbean   Western Pacific   Eastern Mediterranean   Eastern Europe and Central Asia

Source: *Perspectives in Health*, Pan American Health Organization, 2004.
www.paho.org/English/DD/PIN/persp19_box05.htm.

patent will be granted," he says. "If [Combivir] is patented, you might as well shut shop and grant every patent on earth."

Public Interest Groups Step Forward

Earlier this year a number of public-interest groups, including Doctors Without Borders, filed a motion to oppose Glaxo's India patent application. If the patent is granted, Cipla could be required to pay standard 4% royalties to Glaxo, although Menghaney points out that the company could ask for much more. In South Africa, Glaxo demanded a royalty rate of 30% before being challenged by activist groups.

The same coalition also filed a motion to oppose the patenting of another antiretroviral, Viread, which is made by Gilead, a California company. The drug, the groups claim, is merely a crystalline version of an existing medicine. Gilead spokeswoman Amy Flood says, "Viread represents innovation and is patentable under Indian law." The company, she adds, "will use this patent responsibly and won't block access to our medication in India or in other resource-limited countries where the HIV epidemic has hit the hardest."

For the past two years, since the government unveiled plans for a free nationwide antiretroviral-therapy program for people with AIDS, India has bought its drugs from generic-pharmaceutical makers such as Cipla and Ranbaxy. Although at least 500,000 Indians have full-blown AIDS, enrollment in the free-drug program is fewer than 35,000. "We have been going forward in a slow, guarded manner," says A.K. Khera, who is in charge of AIDS drug therapy for India's Health Ministry. "Now we are scaling up and going to expand in a very big way."

The ramping-up of government-provided treatment —India will spend about $5.6 million on antiretrovirals this year—coincides with the campaign by Western pharmaceutical companies to pursue patents and royalties for their inventions. That's what worries activists like Anand Grover, who works with the Lawyers Collective in Mumbai, which is spearheading the campaign against the Combivir and Viread patents. "Decisions made by Indian patent offices are a question of life or death for people with AIDS," he says. "They rely on the availability of affordable drugs and other essential medicines made by Indian generics manufacturers."

Glaxo sees things differently. "The challenge of HIV," it said in a statement, "needs to be tackled through intensive communication and education. The root cause of a country's inability to address its health-care problem does not lie with patents but with inadequate health-care infrastructure and funds."

A decision in the Combivir case is expected this fall. But other battles are just gearing up. About 9,000 patents have been filed in India by Western drug companies since 1995, all of them piled up in the so-called patent office mailbox. An estimated 1,000 of them are now under review. "There are hundreds of patents like this in the mailbox, and there will be many more challenges, especially with AIDS drugs," says Cipla's Hamied, who suggests companies withdraw many of the patents they have filed. "And who profits? Only the lawyers."

Mandatory HIV Testing in the United States Will Curb AIDS

Bernadine Healy

In the following article, Bernadine Healy claims that mandatory AIDS testing should be required for everyone in the United States between the ages of thirteen and sixty-four. Testing is necessary because HIV is spreading to around forty-two thousand people a year in the United States, and a quarter of all HIV-positive people do not even know that they are infected.

Dr. Bernadine Healy is health editor for *U.S. News & World Report* and writes the *On Health* column. She is a member of the President's Council of Advisors on Science and Technology and has served as director of the National Institutes of Health and as president and chief executive officer of the American Red Cross.

Last Friday [December 1, 2006] was World AIDS Day. People across the planet held hands in solidarity against a lethal microbe hellbent on finding a

SOURCE: Bernadine Healy, "AIDS: We're Not There Yet," *U.S. News & World Report*, vol. 141, December 11, 2006, p. 86. Copyright © 2006 U.S. News and World Report, L.P. All rights reserved. Reprinted with permission.

warm human body in which to incubate, replicate, and from which to transmit itself to others. The HIV virus has killed 25 million people since its appearance in 1981; today, at least 40 million people worldwide are infected. The awareness day stems from a United Nations initiative (its slogan: "Keep the Promise") intended to help nations cope with the epidemic. Governments, private foundations, and corporations have committed billions of dollars to make the highly active anti-retroviral drugs, which can turn AIDS into a chronic manageable disease, available to poorer nations. The promise is powerful, especially if one looks at how the drugs have transformed the face of AIDS in the United States. But there's something odd going on: Despite the commendable enthusiasm for helping victims beyond our borders, a strange complacency has set in at home. Many people think the new blockbuster drugs have solved the AIDS problem. They're wrong. HIV is alive and well in America and spreading vigorously, with 42,000 new cases of HIV infection a year.

FAST FACT

Of more than 40 million people living with AIDS, upwards of 90 percent are unaware of their infections, according to the Clinton Foundation.

To be sure, the obituary pages are no longer filled with the names of AIDS victims. The infected are living long and productive lives with survival times exceeding 20 years or more. The sick don't look so sick either, though drug side effects can be debilitating. And the practice of AIDS medicine is mostly about outpatient visits, focused on the doctor determining just the right level of drugs to suppress the virus in the patient's blood to undetectable levels. This is far from the crisis medicine of years gone by that still prevails in poorer parts of the world: overwhelming pneumonia and septic shock, heart failure and dementia, rotting gums and emaciated bodies.

Unchecked, the disease moves swiftly with a looming threat of death so powerful that AIDS doctors even

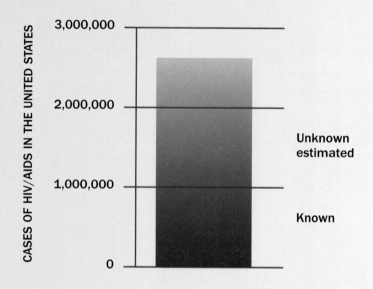

Known and Projected HIV/AIDS Cases in the United States, 2006

CASES OF HIV/AIDS IN THE UNITED STATES

3,000,000

2,000,000

1,000,000

0

Unknown estimated

Known

Source: Twenty-Five Years of AIDS—United States, 1981–2006. www.cdc.gov/mmwr/preview/mmwrhtml/mm552a1.htm. June 2, 2006.

through the mid-'90s felt they were on a battlefield, says Jerome Groopman, a professor of medicine at Harvard and an AIDS expert. That's not so today but, Groopman adds, the medical problems are just as important. For one thing, about 25 percent of patients are becoming resistant to the multiple antiviral drugs in use. So far, the pharmaceutical pipeline has been able to churn out new drugs in the nick of time. And the needs are great, since 1.2 million Americans are infected by the virus, and the number is growing.

A study in the current issue of the *American Journal of Pathology* by scientists at Inserm, France's version of the National Institutes of Health, highlights the ongoing threat. Semen is the prime fluid that transmits HIV to others. The researchers show that testicular tissue is a welcoming site for viral replication, an important finding since the testis is known to be a pharmacological sanctuary that blocks entry of the high-powered antiviral drugs that so effectively penetrate and suppress the virus in other parts of the body. Thus, treated men may feel great and have virtually no virus in their blood, but they can still disseminate lethal semen if they engage in unprotected sex.

Americans Are Not Getting the Message

Despite relentless abstinence campaigns, endless preaching about safe sex, and the condoms delivered with pizza on many a college campus, the National Center for Health Statistics reports that some 14 million Americans flunk

The OraQuick ADVANCE test for HIV provides accurate results in twenty minutes. (**AP Images**)

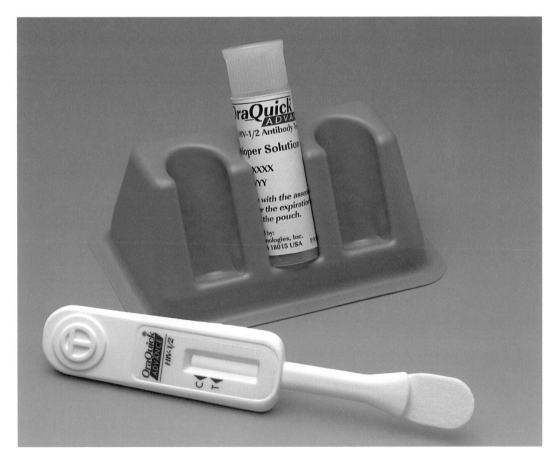

Social Disease 101—by engaging in sexual practices and drug use that put them at risk for HIV. Chlamydia is a good measure of this. In the United States, there are an estimated 2.8 million new cases annually of this highly infectious sexually transmitted disease (which causes pelvic inflammation that can lead to infertility in women). That's an awful lot of young people who are having unprotected sex.

An added problem is that a quarter of those who contract HIV don't even know it. This dilemma has led to a recent turnaround by the Centers for Disease Control and Prevention on routine HIV population screening. In the past, this was a big no-no, since a positive test brought only social stigma and a death sentence. The new guidelines, calling for everyone ages 13 to 64 to be screened for the virus, allows for earlier and more effective treatment. And the screening will uncover several hundred thousand silent HIV carriers who account for over half of the nation's new cases each year. The World Health Organization chimed in last week [December 2006] with a similar proposal.

Sure, testing will no doubt scare people, but maybe that's a good thing. Fear might be the best way to counteract complacency, not to mention the risky impulses that often trump the best of promises.

Mandatory HIV Testing in the United States Is Too Expensive

Sherry Boschert

The Centers for Disease Control and Prevention (CDC) is now recommending universal screening for everyone in the United States aged thirteen to sixty-four. Sherry Boschert, author of the following article, claims that this would identify between 56,000 and 250,000 new cases of HIV/AIDS, which would cost $900 million or more for treatment and counseling. The funds, says Boschert, are not there and neither are the health-care providers. Boschert points out that doctors are reluctant to enter HIV/AIDS care because clinicians in this field are overworked and underfunded.

Sherry Boschert has been an award-winning medical news reporter in the San Francisco bureau of the International Medical News Group since 1991.

New recommendations to test routinely for HIV in all patients aged 13–64 years will overburden the U.S. health care system with newly diagnosed patients unless additional funding is provided, experts said at a press briefing by the Centers for Disease Control and Prevention.

The CDC now recommends "opt-out" testing in which HIV screening is incorporated into routine health care unless the patient declines to be tested. That could identify 56,000 of the 250,000 U.S. residents who are unaware of their infection, generating a need for greater than $900 million in additional funding for counseling

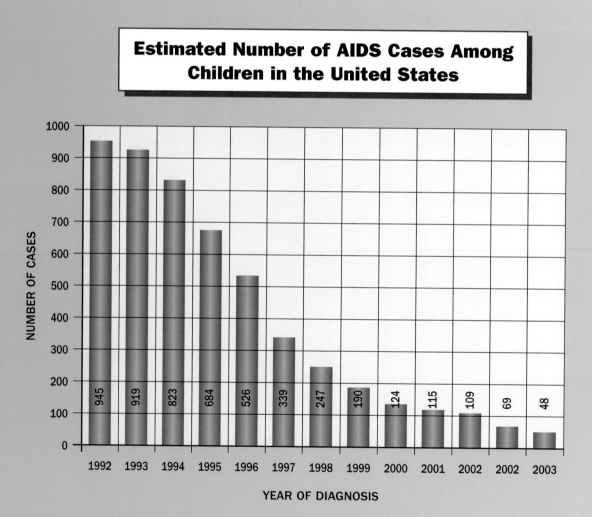

Estimated Number of AIDS Cases Among Children in the United States

YEAR OF DIAGNOSIS

NUMBER OF CASES

1992: 945
1993: 919
1994: 823
1995: 684
1996: 526
1997: 339
1998: 247
1999: 190
2000: 124
2001: 115
2002: 109
2002: 69
2003: 48

Source: Centers for Disease Control and Prevention. www.cdc.gov.hiv/topics/surveillance/resources/reports/2004report/figure1.htm.

and treatment services, said Dr. Kevin Fenton, director of the CDC's National Center for HIV, Sexually Transmitted Diseases, and Tuberculosis Prevention.

He and others spoke at a briefing during a 2-day summit sponsored by the CDC on ways to expand HIV testing and the potential impact of increased numbers of patients diagnosed with HIV.

Approximately 25% of 1.2 million people thought to be living with HIV in the United States are unaware of their infections, the CDC estimates. Dr. Michael Saag, director of the Center for AIDS Research at the University of Alabama, Birmingham, said he believes that 25% may be a low estimate.

> **FAST FACT**
>
> According to the Clinton Foundation, in just the next few years, developing countries will need to test at least 200 million people for HIV, and the costs of testing will be high.

Three-quarters of patients diagnosed with HIV at his clinics have very low CD4 counts, indicating that they probably have been infected for 10–12 years.

Treating the infection early greatly improves survival at 8 years and reduces transmission of the virus. "That screams at us that we should be testing earlier, but with that comes an obligation to provide access to care. At our clinic, we're already at capacity," said Dr. Saag.

His institution collects around $360/patient per year in Ryan White Act funding for HIV care, which provides only about $360,000/year of the $2.1 million needed to care for the 1,400 patients served. "It's not sufficient," he said.

Legislation to renew the Ryan White Act has been stalled in Congress for months, he added.

We Just Cannot Afford It

Clinicians who provide HIV care are among the lowest paid health care providers, Dr. Saag's analyses suggest. People entering health care professions see the overworked

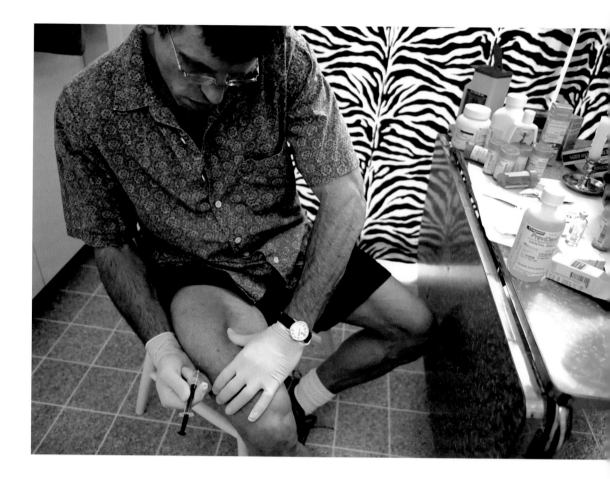

Wesley Lanton injects himself with one of the many drugs he must take to treat his AIDS. Some are concerned that mandatory testing for AIDS will reveal more cases without there being any means to provide for the expensive treatment they require. (Karen Masmauski/Science Faction/Getty Images)

clinicians and underfunded care for patients with HIV and AIDS, and fewer today are interested in working in HIV care in the United States, he said.

At the Johns Hopkins University clinics in Baltimore, most patients with HIV are unemployed, and 45% are uninsured—demographics that are common to other areas of the country, Dr. John S. Bartlett added. Caring for thousands of newly diagnosed HIV infections "will take clinics committed to taking care of the under-served," said Dr. Bartlett, professor of medicine and chief of infectious diseases at the university.

The burden of new diagnoses should not be a barrier to wider HIV testing, the panel emphasized.

To improve screening rates, more than funding will be needed, added Phill Wilson, founder and executive director of the Black AIDS Institute in Los Angeles. People who are unaware of their HIV infection are more likely to be young minorities, particularly African Americans. The stigma of HIV infection must be addressed by mobilizing the black community, he said.

"In an environment where testing is free, painless, quick, and can save someone's life, why are people reluctant to get tested? The debilitating stigma" of AIDS, Mr. Wilson said.

National investment in HIV-prevention programs correlates with the level of new infections over time, according to an analysis by David R. Holtgrave, Ph.D., chair of the school of public health at Johns Hopkins University.

The CDC's current budget of $700 million/year for HIV prevention is about $350 million short of what's needed for comprehensive prevention services, he estimated.

CHAPTER 3

Personal Narratives on AIDS

A Young African Woman Reports on AIDS in Her Lifetime

Suzanne Engo

In this rap piece, Suzanne Engo explores the tension a young girl feels between wanting boys to like her and fearing what having sex could do to her.

In 2003 Suzanne Engo founded the New York AIDS Film Festival, which was launched at the United Nations as the world's first HIV/AIDS film festival. She is taking the early steps toward a larger dream that she has held for some time: to create the New York AIDS Museum, which will serve as an HIV/AIDS memorial and education center.

My story is one among millions of young people who do not remember a time without a computer, MTV or AIDS. When I was very little, my mother sat me down and told me about a pandemic that would eventually become one of the greatest challenges

Photo on facing page. The AIDS Quilt, commemorating those who have died from the disease, covers the National Mall in Washington, D.C.
(AP Images)

SOURCE: Suzanne Engo, "As Long As I Can Remember . . . There's Always Been AIDS: In Memory of Lives Lost in 25 Years of AIDS," *UN Chronicle*, vol. 43, July-August, 2006, pp. 8–9. Copyright © 2006 United Nations. Reprinted with the permission of the United Nations.

and threats my generation would face. What I didn't know was that "as long as I would remember, there would always be AIDS."*

AS LONG AS I CAN REMEMBER, THERE'S ALWAYS BEEN AIDS.

Nobody really talked about it because it only happened to gay people—apparently—and no one really talked about it, but mummy said others could have it too.

AS LONG AS I CAN REMEMBER, THERE'S ALWAYS BEEN AIDS.

In high school, we got condoms and were told all the time to practice safe sex, or AIDS will come in time. There's always temptation, there's always the rest, but put on a rubber, you kids do your best.

The church said no condoms, no sex is the best, just zip up your trousers and don't show your chest. Boys are shame, shame, shame; you get in that business and you'll be to blame. I don't really like boys and they don't seem to care, so long as there's no sex, no AIDS will be there. As for boys and boys I don't really care, behind closed doors I'm not even there.

AS LONG AS I CAN REMEMBER, THERE'S ALWAYS BEEN AIDS.

Magic Johnson has it, he doesn't look sick? Tom Hanks and Denzel, what the hell? What's really going on? What is really being said? It's all over TV and on the news, it seems like this AIDS is getting taboo.

AS LONG AS I CAN REMEMBER, THERE'S ALWAYS BEEN AIDS.

Everyone's tired of hearing about AIDS and condoms too—leave us alone, we know what to do!

AS LONG AS I CAN REMEMBER, THERE'S ALWAYS BEEN AIDS.

I haven't had sex yet, no drugs here. But he pulled down my shorts in a bad way and pushed down my

FAST FACT

By 2004 in the United States, African Americans accounted for 55 percent of HIV infections among individuals aged thirteen to twenty-four.

head. . . . It's crazy to think that the first time is like this, I hope there's no AIDS here, I wish I was dead.

AS LONG AS I CAN REMEMBER, THERE'S ALWAYS BEEN AIDS.

I can't believe I'm almost eighteen, and after all those lectures, I didn't know what to do. He said he forgot the condoms and that he loved me too; I asked about testing and who he'd been with? I know that's not enough, I know it's not true, but finally I'm pretty and boys think so, too.

I can't tell my mum, she'll kill me for sure; she'll throw away the keys and lock up the door. After all that I said and

In one of the most famous examples of an HIV-positive celebrity, basketball star Earvin "Magic" Johnson announces his retirement from the NBA in 1991 because he is HIV-positive. (**AP Images**)

the work that I've done, I made a mistake, my mouth's open wide; I'm such a hypocrite, it's like I have lied. . . .

I know what I'll do, I've got it: I'll wait and give blood —yeah, that's what I'll do, and just as the lady said, if they don't call to say anything, then nothing to fret. Phew, they never called.

AS LONG AS I CAN REMEMBER, THERE'S ALWAYS BEEN AIDS.

I haven't slipped since way back when. God knows, in fear, I learned my lesson then. But now all the time there is news from home (Africa). This one died of a stomach ache, that one of a cold. Nobody says they die of AIDS.

Your village will kill you, your babies won't grow and when your money's all spent, you'll die like an animal and go to hell. Everyone has stories, but nobody knows whether AIDS comes from a virus or it happens when it snows. . . .

AS LONG AS I CAN REMEMBER, THERE'S ALWAYS BEEN AIDS.

Now I'm in college and we heard some campaigns, but nothing about AIDS in America—it's a problem that's just not here. I tell all my friends, take care of yourselves; one mistake in bed and you could be dead. Ooooh, hush, oh stop, we get the point, but when was the last time you saw Magic J. dead?

AS LONG AS I CAN REMEMBER, THERE'S ALWAYS BEEN AIDS.

Now I am a young woman and I've had enough. . . . My Africa is dying and nothing's being said. It's like you can live if you've got the pence but if you ain't got no money, you're gonna be dead.

The campaigns are back and I'm sure glad to see, "wrap it up," said it hip hop, know HIV/AIDS pop, then "think MTV" came and told us fight back. If he says he loves you and you're the best, get on the train and go get a test.

AS LONG AS I CAN REMEMBER, THERE'S AL-WAYS BEEN AIDS.

My favorite person died, my sister is sick, my dance teacher died, that lady from church I heard she passed on. So I'm showing these movies downtown at Quad, they'll show you their stories and urge you to test, when you leave the cinema, you all will know best.

AS LONG AS I CAN REMEMBER, THERE'S AL-WAYS BEEN AIDS.

"We all have HIV/AIDS"—yes, this is true—from Beverly Hills to Ouagadougou, from Bali to Yaounde, Dakar or Japan, around the world this AIDS has spanned: straight, queer, hunters of deer, grey hair, black, botox or not. As long as I have lived, there's always been AIDS, and it will always be there if nothing is changed.

Go back to your village, bungalow, bed; go back to your mission, your courage, your dread. Stop into your pharmacist, classroom, or talk to your board. Since "we all have AIDS" and if nothing is said, it seems quite simple, we all will be dead.

AS LONG AS I CAN REMEMBER, THERE'S AL-WAYS BEEN AIDS.

But there is one thing, and I believe it is true, there's so much fight left in me and in you. We'll care if people are sick here or there, we'll care about dying anywhere.

So when I look back at my life in 25 more years, I'll see bolded in red: Once there was AIDS, it killed many friends, but now it is over, now it is dead.

*For UN Secretary-General Kofi Annan, who told us to "make a noise."

A Young Woman Learns She Is HIV-Positive

Michelle Towner

When she was just fifteen years old, author Michelle Towner tested positive for HIV. Like most teens, contracting HIV was the last thing on her mind when she decided to have sex with her first serious boyfriend. After discovering she was HIV-positive, Michelle was angry, confused, and worried. But after calling an AIDS hotline and talking to a social worker, she learned that she could still live a long, normal life. At age seventeen, Michelle trained to become a peer counselor in order to inform other young people about HIV.

Every hour of every day, two Americans under 20 are infected with HIV. And a lot of girls are contracting it—not from one-night stands, but from longer relationships . . . the way it may have happened to this teen.

SOURCE: Michelle Towner as told to Stephanie Booth, "I'm HIV Positive," *Teen Magazine*, vol. 43, October 1999. Reproduced by permission of the author.

I was 15 when I decided to have sex with Ben, my first serious boyfriend. I worried that I'd get pregnant, not that I'd end up HIV positive. But that's exactly what happened.

I met Ben at the movie theater when I was 14. We ran in different circles because he was three years older than I was, but we liked a lot of the same music and movies and were both big Chicago Bulls fans. Ben was cute and sweet, and things between us got serious fast. When Ben brought up the idea of sex a few months later, it seemed right to me. We were in love.

We used a condom only about half the time we had sex. I knew you could get STDs that way, but Ben told me not to worry, and I trusted him. I knew he was more experienced than I was, so I figured he knew what he was talking about. The thought of HIV never crossed my mind — I would never have suggested we get tested before we had sex.

> **FAST FACT**
>
> Of all the women diagnosed with HIV in the United States in 2005, 80 percent of the cases were transmitted through heterosexual contact.

We dated for a year and a half, until I moved away. My father died when I was younger, and my [mother] and I never got along that great. So I decided to go live in a different section of Chicago with my aunt, who I was very close to. I knew that would mean Ben and I wouldn't see each other as much, and I worried that we'd drift apart.

Soon after the move, we did break up. I was crushed. I went back to my old neighborhood a couple of times, hoping to bump into him, but no one had seen him. I figured he had a new girlfriend, which made me feel even worse.

A Bad Diagnosis

About six months after I moved, I got really sick. I was running a high fever and throwing up, and I didn't have the energy to crawl out of bed for two days. My aunt

This safe-sex kit contains items such as condoms and safe-sex literature. While most Americans are aware of how to protect themselves from HIV and AIDS, many still engage in unsafe sex. (AP Images)

made an appointment for me at the doctor, but she had to work, so I went by myself. While the doctor examined me, he asked one question after another: "Do you drink?" "Do you do drugs?" . . . "Do you smoke?" The answers were all no, until he asked if I'd had unprotected sex. "Just with my boyfriend," I said. He asked if he could test me for HIV, and I was like, "Why not?" I was sure I didn't have it. They took some blood and said to call in a few days for the results. I blew it off because I still felt so sick and just wasn't in the mood.

The nurse wound up calling me and asked me to come back in as soon as possible. I just thought, or hoped, they were going to give me different antibiotics.

The HIV test was still in the back of my mind, though. Then I knew something was wrong when the nurse made me wait in the doctor's private office. By the time the doctor came in, my hands were all clammy and I was shaking. Then he dropped the bomb: "Michelle, you're HIV positive," he said.

My first thought was, "I'm dying." I felt so angry and confused. Then I asked myself, "How did this happen?" "Who gave this to me?" I didn't want to think it was Ben, but I hadn't had sex with anyone else. The doctor asked if there was anyone he could call for me, but I didn't want to tell my aunt. I was too ashamed.

The next week I faked being sick and hid in my bedroom. I worried that everyone at school would suddenly be able to tell I was HIV positive and wouldn't want to come near me, and I was scared that I would accidentally infect someone. Every time my aunt tried to talk to me, I screamed at her to leave me alone. The doctor gave me brochures about HIV, but I was too depressed to read them. I didn't feel like eating or sleeping. I just felt so alone. Then one night, I finally snuck the phone into my room and called an AIDS hotline that was on one of the brochures.

Return to the Living

I felt weird calling, but it was the best thing I could have done. The woman I spoke to that night was so understanding; she didn't preach to me. She referred me to an AIDS clinic, and I went the next day. Neal, a social worker there, gave me a shoulder to cry on. He told me lots of people with positive status live pretty normal lives for a long time, but I had to face up to being sick.

The next time I met with Neal, I brought my aunt. She knew I was seeing someone for depression but didn't know the details. When Neal told her I was HIV positive, my aunt didn't believe it. She demanded I take a second blood test. When that came back positive, she hugged me for what felt like forever. "You have to take care of yourself," she said. My aunt's been so supportive. She helped me break the news to the rest of my family, and she tells them how I'm doing when I don't feel like talking about it.

The doctor gave me medicine, AZT, to take at exact times twice a day. At first it made me tired, and I got monster headaches and stomachaches. The side effects aren't as bad now, but I get sick really easily. I caught my aunt's cold and was in bed for days. Another time, I got dehydrated and was in the hospital for more than a week. A lot of people with HIV lose weight or get bad rashes, and every day I wake up scared to look in the mirror and see those symptoms. I go to the doctor every three months, and each time, I dread bad news—that I have

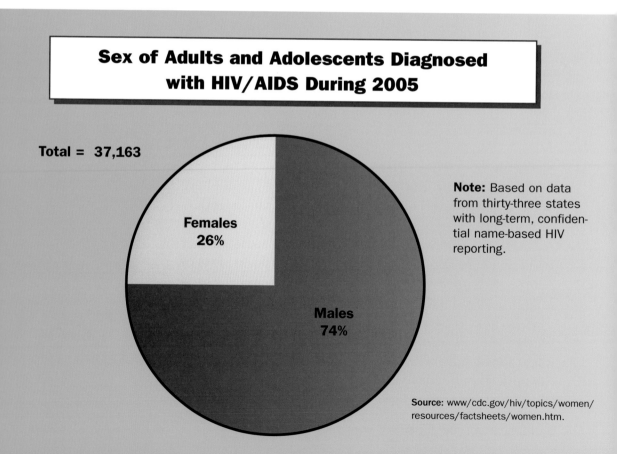

Sex of Adults and Adolescents Diagnosed with HIV/AIDS During 2005

Total = 37,163

Females 26%

Males 74%

Note: Based on data from thirty-three states with long-term, confidential name-based HIV reporting.

Source: www/cdc.gov/hiv/topics/women/resources/factsheets/women.htm.

full-blown AIDS. I'm OK so far, but I'll be on AZT for who knows how long.

I'm trying to keep everything normal, but it feels like everything has changed. Eventually I'm going to have to tell my friends. Keeping this secret is so hard. But what do I say, "Hey, great outfit, and by the way, I'm positive"? I still hide my pills if they come over. Or if we're out and I have to take one, I make an excuse and run to the bathroom. Sleepovers are impossible. I think my friends would understand, but I don't want them to feel sorry for me or think I'm contagious and be scared off.

It's the same with any guy I date. I had a boyfriend, but I didn't let it get too intense. I'm not ready to go there. I kinda push guys away right now. Of course, if I found the right guy, I definitely would tell him before things got serious.

Looking back, I think Ben slept with a lot more girls than he told me about. I guess we should have talked more about sexual history and practiced safe sex all the time. I'll never know whether or not he knew he was HIV positive. He's moved away, and I've moved on. I'm 17 now and training to be a peer counselor so I can talk to other kids about HIV. At least I have a chance to warn others. Each day I'm alive gives me another opportunity to get the word out.

An American Wife and Mother Copes with AIDS

Nell Casey

Author Nell Casey tells the story of Dawn Averitt Bridge, a young woman who always wanted a marriage and children. At nineteen, however, she was raped and infected with HIV. Doctors cautioned her against becoming pregnant because at that time the rate of mother-to-child infection was at least 70 percent. But soon after she progressed to full-blown AIDS, the new antiretroviral drugs became available and gave Dawn a chance to experience the life she had always desired. Nell Casey's articles have appeared in *Elle, Mirabella, Salon*, and the *New York Times Book Review*.

At a small preschool in rural Virginia, in a corridor lined with kids' colorful, cheery drawings, Dawn Averitt Bridge is chatting with one of her daughters' teachers. Dawn's girls—the copper-haired Maddy, 4,

SOURCE: Nell Casey, "A Mom—Not a Victim: A Devastating Diagnosis Seemed to End Her Dream of Having a Big Family. Then Medical Advances Turned Her Life Around. How Dawn Averitt Bridge Is Meeting the Challenges of Parenting with AIDS," *Good Housekeeping*, vol. 244, February 2007, pp. 99–101. Copyright © 2007 Hearst Communications. Reproduced by permission of the author.

and the blond cherub Sophie, 2—dart in and out of her legs as she talks; when Sophie stops, briefly, to give her mother a hug, she gets a bright smile and an affectionate caress in return. It's an ordinary scene, though Dawn, 38, never takes ordinary for granted. She knows how lucky she is to be here, to have this moment.

It Can Happen to Any Girl

At 19, in 1988, Dawn contracted HIV, the virus that causes AIDS. At the time, the diagnosis was considered a death sentence. People with AIDS were thought to have a life expectancy of less than a year, and HIV-positive women were cautioned against trying to have kids: Dawn was told that her chances of infecting a baby would be between 70 and 100 percent. Pregnancy was also believed to speed the course of the disease. "Honestly, not having children felt worse than death to me." Dawn recalls. "Dying seemed so abstract. But I had always wanted kids, for as long as I could remember."

Earlier that year, Dawn had decided to take time off from college to live in Spain. A week after she arrived in Madrid, a man broke into her room at a youth hostel and raped her. Dawn hid in her room for days after. When she emerged, she went into complete denial, repressing the details of the attack for years. "I still don't talk about it much," she says. "I don't want to be thought of as a victim. The message to take from the rape isn't, That won't happen to me so I don't need to worry about it. It's that you never know: Sometimes it takes only one exposure to get infected."

Dawn returned home to Atlanta with severely swollen lymph nodes. With her mom, a nurse, by her side, she spent three weeks visiting specialists, having blood taken for tests, trying to figure out what was wrong. Finally—just as a doctor was about to order a biopsy to check for non-Hodgkin's lymphoma—Dawn requested an HIV test. The doctor advised against it (he thought the test would look bad on her medical record), but Dawn insisted: people she knew were starting to talk about AIDS. "Everyone thought this was a gay man's disease," Dawn remembers. "And I was a middle-class white girl from the South who'd never even smoked a cigarette." When that test and a follow-up both came back positive, doctors discouraged her from telling anyone: The stigma, they said, would be too great.

> **FAST FACT**
>
> From 1992 to 2005, the number of children infected yearly with HIV during pregnancy in the United States dropped from 855 to 57.

Dawn transferred from New York University to Georgia State to be near her family (her parents and two brothers were the only ones who knew about the diagnosis). She moved into an apartment and bought a dog to replace the children she'd been told she'd never have. A couple of years after graduation, she started work as an AIDS activist, and by 1995, at 26, Dawn was running her own nonprofit advocacy group, the first of its kind to focus on information about treatment for women with HIV/AIDS.

Fighting for Life

But by then her T cell count—the number of a certain kind of infection-fighting white blood cell—had fallen dangerously low. Her disease had progressed to full-blown AIDS, and her condition was worsening. Knowing it might be her last chance, Dawn had fought her way into a clinical trial for a new class of drugs called protease inhibitors. Almost immediately after she started the medication, her T cell count returned to a healthy level. By 1996, her overall health had rebounded.

Dawn's reaction to the drugs was not unique: Protease inhibitors seemed to be the medical miracle doctors had been searching for. "People were climbing out of their deathbeds and getting their lives together again," Dawn recalls. In 1997, AIDS fell out of the top 10 causes of death in the United States, where it had appeared since

1990. (Even now, though, it isn't known how long the drugs can remain effective.)

For the first time since she was 19, Dawn was able to imagine having a family. "I realized that maybe it wasn't impossible to think about children," she says. The following year, she met Brad Bridge, then a 27-year-old computer specialist, and with a renewed sense of hope, she gave herself over to a serious relationship with him. As the two grew closer, Dawn worried that Brad might not truly grasp the severity of her illness. "You understand that there is a chance I could die," she pressed him more than once, "and, if we have kids, you could end up a single parent?"

"I understand," Brad always answered. They were married in August 2001.

Six-week-old infant Jomalier Diaz lies in his crib in Puerto Rico. Because his mother is HIV-positive, he is receiving treatment with the drug AZT in an attempt to prevent him from contracting the disease from her. (AP Images)

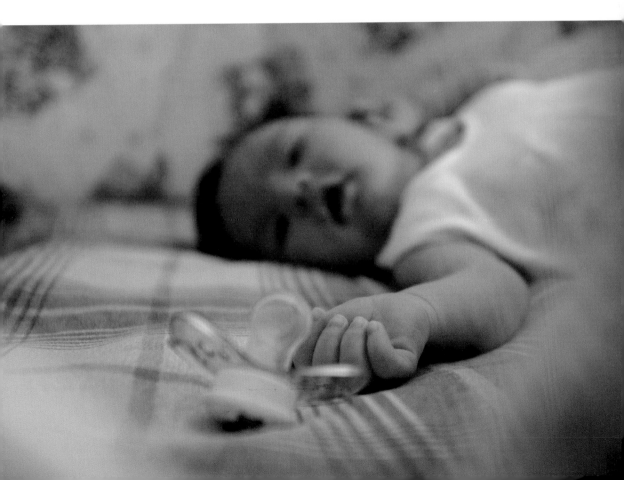

"He is my rock, my foundation," Dawn says now. "With him, I can be scared and have hard days and grapple with everything that this disease brings up." Two months after the wedding, Dawn was pregnant—and the couple was ecstatic. "I just didn't believe it," she says. "I must have done eight pregnancy tests over the course of four days. Being pregnant meant that I was not only living my life, I was also creating life. I was prevailing."

Dawn and Brad practice safe sex, and Brad is HIV-negative. Dawn won't discuss how they conceived, but HIV-positive couples generally use one of two methods: home insemination with a needle-less syringe, or in vitro fertilization at a clinic. By the time Dawn got pregnant, the risk of a reasonably healthy HIV-positive woman passing the disease to her baby had dropped to between 1 and 2 percent. By then it was also known that pregnancy does not accelerate the progression of HIV in the mother. Dawn's most pressing concern was that her baby might be born prematurely, which can be a risk for women with HIV.

The Children She Longed For

On June 29, 2002, after a grueling 27-hour labor, Dawn gave birth to a healthy baby girl, whom she and Brad named Madelyn Grace (Maddy). Dawn had planned to deliver vaginally—which many experts consider medically safe for HIV-positive women in good health—but ended up having an emergency cesarean section because Maddy was in the wrong position. But the birth "was, hands down, the most amazing experience of my life," Dawn recalls, eyes brimming with tears. "When we brought her home, I would go in to see her in her crib and I would drop to my knees and think, Oh please let me see her grow up. HIV became real for me the day she was born. My fear of dying and my desire to survive became palpable."

Dawn had always wanted a big family, and she soon got pregnant again, even though she feared she might be tempting fate. "Once I had Maddy, this miracle baby, I wondered, How could I think about another?" she says. But on February 26, 2004, Dawn delivered a second beautiful baby girl, Sophia Alston (Sophie), in a planned C-section.

Several months must pass before doctors can be absolutely certain that a baby is HIV-negative. So as a preventive measure, Dawn made the difficult decision to give each of her girls a four-to-six-week course of the drug AZT, which has been proven to lower the risk of contracting HIV. AZT is a potent drug, and administering it to an infant proved more wrenching than Dawn had expected. "Every six hours, 24 hours a day, I had to go in with a dropper full of medicine and have this little newborn suck it down," she says. She admitted to Brad that it was too much for her, and, she remembers, "he just said, 'I can do this.' And from then on, he did."

Both girls were tested for HIV three times: as newborns, at 6 months, and then at 18 months. "That first year, every time the baby would get a cough, an ear infection, a fever, there was no way for my heart not to go, Oh my God, please no—don't let this be it," Dawn says. "And then the day the doctor calls and says, 'The last HIV test is here, everything is OK'—it's amazing. To me, there is no greater privilege than to be the mother of these children." Dawn did forgo breastfeeding, because there is still a 15 to 25 percent chance of an HIV-positive mother infecting her baby through nursing.

Facing the Future

The family now lives in Nellysford, VA, where Dawn and Brad are building a house on a sprawling, grassy plot of land. Dawn knows that she will have to talk honestly to her children about her health once they are old enough to understand. "I want to demonstrate to my kids that there is nothing to be ashamed of," she says. "They should always be able to speak proudly of who they are." She is still very active in AIDS causes, chairing the board of the Well Project (thewellproject.org), a nonprofit she founded for women with HIV/AIDS, as well as working on the Grace Study, a large U.S. trial focusing on treatment for women with HIV. She jokes that someday she'd like to start a national HIV-positive soccer mom association: "We could fill quite a lot of minivans, let me tell you!"

Now, with the 20th anniversary of her diagnosis approaching, Dawn remains healthy. Even so, there is no road map for people like her. She is part of the first generation to live with AIDS as a chronic condition. "We no longer know the prognosis for this illness," says Jane Hitti, M.D., associate professor of obstetrics and gynecology at the University of Washington School of Medicine and an AIDS researcher. "I tell my patients with HIV, 'You can live with this for a long time. There is a good chance you will see your baby graduate from high school.'"

The most difficult days for Dawn are when she hears that someone she knows with HIV—someone she has recently seen and admired for her robust health—has suddenly died. And yet Dawn has always managed to stay one step ahead of her illness. "I am unwilling for this to overtake me," she says. "I take my meds. I do what I have to do to stay well. I have so much to accomplish, with my kids and in life. I'm just not willing to be done."

GLOSSARY

acute retroviral syndrome	A group of symptoms resembling mononucleosis that often are the first sign of HIV infection in 50 to 70 percent of all patients and 45 to 90 percent of women.
AIDS dementia complex	A type of brain dysfunction caused by HIV infection that causes difficulty thinking, confusion, and loss of muscular coordination.
antibody	A specific protein produced by the immune system in response to a specific foreign protein or particle, called an antigen.
antigen	Any substance that stimulates the body to produce an antibody.
autoimmunity	A condition in which the body's immune system produces antibodies in response to its own tissues or blood components instead of foreign particles or microorganisms.
control	See *placebo*.
efficacy trial	See *Phase 3 vaccine trial*.
HIV	Human immunodeficiency virus; a transmissible retrovirus that causes AIDS in humans. Two forms of HIV are now recognized: HIV-1, which causes most cases of AIDS in Europe, North and South America, and most parts of Africa; and HIV-2, which is chiefly found in West African patients. HIV-2, discovered in 1986, appears to be less virulent than HIV-1 and may also have a longer latency period.
human immunodeficiency virus	See *HIV*.
immunodeficiency	A condition in which the body's immune response is damaged, weakened, or is not functioning properly.

immunogenicity	The ability of an antigen or vaccine to stimulate immune response.
Kaposi's sarcoma	A cancer of the connective tissue that produces painless purplish red (in people with light skin) or brown (in people with dark skin) blotches on the skin. It is a major diagnostic mark of AIDS.
latent period	Also called the incubation period, this is the time between infection with a disease-causing agent and the development of the disease.
lymphocyte	A type of white blood cell that is important in the formation of antibodies. It can be used to monitor the health of AIDS patients because HIV destroys lymphocytes.
mycobacterium avium infection (MAC)	A type of opportunistic infection that occurs in about 40 percent of AIDS patients and is regarded as an AIDS-defining disease.
non-nucleoside reverse transcriptase inhibitor	The newest class of antiretroviral drugs, which work by inhibiting the reverse transcriptase enzyme necessary for HIV replication.
nucleoside analogues	The first group of effective antiretroviral medications. They interfere with the synthesis of DNA by the AIDS virus.
opportunistic infection	An infection by organisms that usually do not cause infection in people whose immune systems are working normally.
Phase 1 vaccine trial	A closely monitored clinical trial of a vaccine conducted in a small number of healthy volunteers. A Phase 1 trial is designed to determine the vaccine's safety in humans, its metabolism and pharmacological actions, and side effects associated with increasing doses.
Phase 2 vaccine trial	A controlled clinical study of a vaccine to identify common short-term side effects and risks associated with the vaccine and to collect information on its immunogenicity. Phase 2 trials enroll some volunteers who have the same characteristics as

persons who would be enrolled in a Phase 3 trial of a vaccine. Phase 2 trials enroll up to several hundred participants.

Phase 3 vaccine trial A large controlled study to determine the ability of a vaccine to produce a desired clinical effect on the risk of a given infection, disease, or other clinical condition at an optimally selected dose and schedule. These trials also gather additional information about safety needed to evaluate the overall benefit/risk relationship of the vaccine and to provide an adequate basis for labeling. Phase 3 trials usually include several hundred to several thousand volunteers.

placebo An inactive substance administered to some study participants while others receive the agent under evaluation. This procedure, also called a control, provides a basis for comparison of effects.

Pneumocystis carinii pneumonia (PCP) An opportunistic infection caused by a fungus that is a major cause of death in patients with late-stage AIDS.

prime-boost In HIV vaccine research, administration of one type of vaccine, such as a live-vector vaccine, followed by or together with a second type of vaccine, such as a recombinant subunit vaccine. The intent of this combination regimen is to induce certain immune responses that will be enhanced by the booster dose.

progressive multifocal leukoencephalopathy (PML) A disease caused by a virus that destroys white matter in localized areas of the brain. It is regarded as an AIDS-defining illness.

protease inhibitors The second major category of drugs used to treat AIDS. It works by suppressing the replication of the AIDS virus.

retrovirus A virus that contains a unique enzyme called reverse transcriptase, which allows it to replicate within new host cells.

T cells Lymphocytes that regulate the immune system's response to infections, including HIV.

wasting syndrome A progressive loss of weight and muscle tissue caused by the AIDS virus.

CHRONOLOGY

1959   The oldest specimen of the AIDS virus, now identified as HIV, is detected in a blood sample donated by a man in Leopoldville, Congo.

1980   Doctors begin to notice unusual diseases, such as *Pneumocystis carinii pneumonia* and Kaposi's sarcoma, among homosexual men.

1982   AIDS is defined for the first time; scientists agree to call the disease acquired immune deficiency syndrome (AIDS). The three modes of AIDS transmission are identified: blood, mother to child, and sexual intercourse.

1983   In France, Dr. Luc Montagnier isolates the AIDS virus.

In central Africa, a heterosexual AIDS epidemic is reported.

1984   Dr. Robert Gallo identifies the human immuno-deficiency virus (HIV) as the cause of AIDS.

1985   At least one case of AIDS is reported in every country in the world.

The first HIV antibody tests are made available in the United States and Europe.

Screening of blood donations for blood banks begins in the United States and Europe. The first international conference on AIDS is held in Atlanta, Georgia.

Actor Rock Hudson dies of AIDS, bringing the disease to widespread public attention.

President Ronald Reagan mentions AIDS publicly for the first time.

1986 A large trial of the drug AZT as a treatment for AIDS is stopped because the drug appears to be too effective to withhold from patients.

1987 Africa's first community-based response to AIDS, the AIDS Support Organization, is formed in Uganda. It becomes a role model for similar groups around the world.

The World Health Organization (WHO) establishes the Special Programme on AIDS.

AIDS becomes the first disease ever debated on the floor of the UN General Assembly.

AZT is approved for use in the United States.

1988 WHO declares December 1 International AIDS Day.

1990 One million children have lost one or both parents to AIDS.

1991 The red ribbon becomes an international symbol of AIDS awareness.

The anti-HIV drug Virex is launched.

1992–1993 HIV infection in Uganda and Thailand begins to decrease as a result of countrywide campaigns against the disease.

1994–1995 The drugs Zerit and Epivir are launched, increasing the choice of HIV treatments.

1996   The Joint UN Programme on HIV/AIDS (UNAIDS) is launched.

The efficacy of highly active antiretroviral therapy (HAART) is announced at the Eleventh International AIDS Conference.

1997   Supported by UNAIDS, the first public antiretroviral therapy program in Africa, the Drug Access Initiative, is launched first in Uganda, then in Côte d'Ivoire.

1998   Thirty-nine pharmaceutical companies file a lawsuit against the South African government to contest legislation intended to reduce the price of HIV drugs.

1999   The first efficacy trial of an HIV vaccine starts in Thailand.

2000   Five top drug companies agree to slash the price of HIV/AIDS treatment for developing countries; UNAIDS and WHO announce a joint initiative, the Accelerating Access Initiative, with these five pharmaceutical companies to increase access to HIV treatment in the developing world.

2001   The first UN General Assembly Special Session on HIV/AIDS unanimously adopts the Declaration of Commitment on HIV/AIDS, declaring AIDS a global catastrophe and calling for worldwide commitment to fight the disease.

The World Trade Organization adopts the Doha Declaration, calling for wider access to HIV treatment through generic drugs.

2002   The Global Fund to Fight AIDS, Tuberculosis, and Malaria is founded.

2003   President George W. Bush announces the $15 billion President's Emergency Plan for AIDS Relief during his State of the Union Address.

WHO and UNAIDS launch the "3 by 5" initiative to help low- and middle-income countries increase the number of people who have access to antiretroviral therapy to 3 million by the end of 2005.

2004   Researchers announce that a cheap three-in-one generic AIDS pill is as effective as more expensive drugs and should be used in developing countries.

UNAIDS launches the Global Coalition of Women and AIDS.

2005   At the UN 2005 World Summit, World leaders agree to take action to increase HIV prevention, treatment, care, and support, with the aim of coming as close as possible to the goal of universal access to treatment by 2010. By the end of 2005, 1.3 million people in low- and middle-income countries are receiving access to antiretroviral therapy.

2006   Ten million Africans are infected with HIV. Eighteen million have already died from the virus. One in four children in southern Africa has been orphaned. Forty-three million more Africans will die of AIDS by 2010.

2007   WHO reports that "lower prices for HIV drugs significantly improved access to treatment for people in poor countries, but figures are still far off target for the United Nations' long-term goal of universal coverage by 2010."

ORGANIZATIONS TO CONTACT

The editors have compiled the following list of organizations concerned with the issues debated in this book. The descriptions are derived from materials provided by the organizations. All have publications or information available for interested readers. Most of these publications are available online and can be downloaded for free in HTML or PDF format. The list was compiled on the date of publication of the present volume; the information provided here may change. Be aware that many organizations take several weeks or longer to respond to inquiries, so allow as much time as possible.

AIDSinfo
PO Box 6303
Rockville, MD
20849-6303
(800) HIV-0440 or
(301) 519-0459
http://aidsinfo.nih.
gov/

AIDSinfo is a service of the U.S. Department of Health and Human Services. It provides information about HIV/AIDS treatment, prevention, and research.

The AIDS Institute
University of South
Florida College of
Medicine
17 Davis Blvd.,
Suite 403
Tampa, FL 33606
(813) 258-5929
fax: (813) 258-5939
www.theaidsinstitute.
org

The AIDS Institute promotes action for social change through public policy research, advocacy, and community education. It is a leading national agency affiliated with the Division of Infectious Diseases and Tropical Medicine at the University of South Florida College of Medicine.

American Foundation for AIDS Research (amfAR)
120 Wall St.,
13th Floor
New York, NY
10005-3908
(212) 806-1600
fax: (212) 806-1601
www.amfar.org

The American Foundation for AIDS Research supports AIDS prevention and research and advocates AIDS-related public policy. Founded in 1985, amfAR is dedicated to ending the global AIDS epidemic through innovative research and publishes several monographs, compendiums, journals, and periodic publications.

Centers for Disease Control and Prevention (CDC)
1600 Clifton Rd.
Atlanta, GA 30333
(800) 311-3435
www.cdc.gov

The CDC is the nation's premier health promotion, prevention, and preparedness agency and a global leader in public health. It stands at the forefront of public health efforts to prevent and control infectious and chronic diseases, injuries, workplace hazards, disabilities, and environmental health threats.

Food and Drug Administration (FDA)
5600 Fishers Ln.
Rockville, MD 20857-0001
(888) 463-6332
www.fda.gov

The U.S. Food and Drug Administration is responsible for protecting the public health by assuring the safety, efficacy, and security of human and veterinary drugs, biological products, medical devices, the nation's food supply, cosmetics, and products that emit radiation. The FDA helps to speed innovations that make medicines and foods more effective, safer, and more affordable, and it helps members of the public get the accurate information they need to use medicines and foods to improve their health.

Gay Men's Health Crisis
119 W. 24th St.
New York, NY 10011
(212) 367-1000
www.gmhc.org

Founded in 1982, the Gay Men's Health Crisis provides support services, education, and advocacy for men, women, and children with AIDS. The group produces the cable television news show *Living with AIDS* and publishes various brochures as well as *Treatment Fact Sheets*, the periodical newsletters *Lesbian AIDS Project* and *Notes*, and the monthly newsletter *Treatment Issues*, which discusses experimental AIDS therapies.

Joint United Nations Programme on HIV/AIDS (UNAIDS)
UNAIDS Secretariat
20 Avenue Appia
CH-1211 Geneva 27
Switzerland
+41.22.791.3666
www.unaids.org/en/

The Joint United Nations Programme on HIV/AIDS brings together the efforts and resources of ten UN system organizations to the global AIDS response.

The National AIDS Fund
729 15th St. NW,
9th Floor
Washington, DC
20005-1511
(202) 408-4848 or
(888) 234-AIDS
fax: (202) 408-1818
www.aidsfund.org

The National AIDS Fund seeks to eliminate HIV as a major health and social problem. Its members work in partnership with the public and private sectors to provide care and to prevent new infections in communities and in the workplace by means of advocacy, grants, research, and education. The fund also publishes an online newsletter, which is available through its Web site.

National Institute of Allergy and Infectious Diseases (NIAID)
NIAID Office of
Communications
and Public Liaison
6610 Rockledge Dr.,
MSC 6612
Bethesda, MD
20892-6612
(301) 496-5717
www3.niaid.nih.gov/

The NIAID is a branch of the National Institutes of Health. It conducts research and provides public information on HIV/AIDS, among many other health problems.

World Health Organization (WHO)
Department of HIV/AIDS
20 Avenue Appia
CH-1211 Geneva 27
Switzerland
www.who.int/en/

The World Health Organization is the UN's specialized agency for health. WHO's objective, as set out in its constitution, is the attainment by all peoples of the highest possible level of health.

FOR FURTHER READING

Books

Greg Behrman, *The Invisible People*. New York: Free Press, 2004.

Chris Bull, ed., *While the World Sleeps*. New York: Thunder's Mouth, 2003.

Catherine Campbell, *Letting Them Die*. Bloomington: Indiana University Press, 2003.

Melissa Fay Greene, *There Is No Me Without You*. New York: Bloomsbury USA, 2006.

Susan S. Hunter, *AIDS in America*. New York: Palgrave Macmillan, 2006.

———, *AIDS in Asia: A Continent in Peril*. New York: Palgrave Macmillan, 2004.

Stephen Lewis, *Race Against Time*. Toronto, Ontario, Canada: Anasi, 2006.

Randy Shilts, *And the Band Played On: Politics, People, and the AIDS Epidemic*. New York: St. Martin's, 1987.

Gerald J. Stine. *AIDS Update*, 2005. San Francisco: Pearson Education, 2005.

Periodicals

Advocate, "HIV Under Attack," March 27, 2007.

Lawrence K. Altman, "AIDS Is on the Rise Worldwide, U.N. Finds," *New York Times*, November 22, 2006.

Hazel Barrett, "Too Little, Too Late: Response to the HIV/AIDS Epidemics in Sub-Saharan Africa," *Geography*, Summer 2007.

Natasha Bolognesi, "AIDS in Africa: A Question of Trust," *Nature*, October 12, 2006.

Lisa McArthur Daly, Benedicta Mduma, and Dulle Robert, "Njoo Tuzungumze! Come, Let's Talk! A Comprehensive Program Seeks to Change Behavior and Promote HIV Counseling and Testing in Tanzania," *Communication World*, January/February 2007.

Economist, "Blood Debts," January 20, 2007.

———, "A Sickness of the Soul," September 9, 2006.

Stephan Faris, "Calling All Healers," *Time*, July 24, 2006.

Carlotta Gall, "A New Sorrow for Afghanistan," *New York Times*, March 19, 2007.

Kenslea Ged and Lori Yeghiayan, "AIDS Treatment Goes Global," *USA Today Magazine*, March 2006.

Christine Gorman, "The Graying of AIDS," *Time*, August 14, 2006.

Peter Griffiths and Alison Paul, "The Bigger Picture: Nanomedicines May Be Small-Scale, but They Offer Huge Potential," *Chemistry and Industry*, January 2, 2006.

Fred Guterl, "Dealing with the Disease," *Newsweek*, August 15, 2005.

Claudia Kalb and Andrew Murr, "Battling a Black Epidemic," *Newsweek*, May 15, 2006.

Michael D. Lemonick and Alice Park, "Vaccines Stage a Comeback," *Time*, January 21, 2002.

Digby Lidstone, "A Stark Warning: The Middle East Has the Lowest Rates of HIV/AIDS of Any Region in the World, but It Is Also One of the Most Vulnerable . . . and Infection Rates Are Climbing Fast," *Middle East Economic Digest*, February 10, 2006.

Coco Masters, "The Thin Blue Line," *Time*, November 21, 2005.

Sylvester Monroe, "Personal Journeys of Women with HIV/AIDS," *Ebony*, December 2006.

Newsweek, "AIDS: Twenty-Five Years Later," May 15, 2006.

Rai Saritha, "Sex, Money, and Power in India," *Time*, March 20, 2006.

John Simons, "Crunch Time for an HIV Test," *Fortune*, May 29, 2006.

INDEX

A

ABC principles, 80–81

Acute retroviral syndrome, 16–17

Africa

AIDS hinders security in, 68–69

AIDS victims in, 53

antiretroviral drugs will curb AIDS, 83–89

herpes/poverty and, 71–76

percent of HIV-infected individuals in, 73

percent of people with untreated STDs in, 72

reasons for spread of HIV in, 73–74

traditions and AIDS, 77–82

See also Sub-Saharan Africa

AIDS (acquired immune deficiency syndrome), 12

advance in science of, 39

current drug therapies for, 25–31, 83–89

in developing world, 45–55

moral obligation to fight, 56–62

diagnosis of, 20, 22

epidemic in Africa

antiretroviral drugs curb, 83–89

herpes/poverty are responsible, 71–76

personal narrative on, 107–12

traditional behavior and, 77–82

first U.S. victims of, 7

global deaths from, 39, 41

narrative of mother with, 118–24

new and projected cases in U.S., 98

psychological impact of, 29–31

typical stages of, 16–19

AIDS dementia complex, 19

AIDS treatment

Brazil's efforts at, 92

drug cocktails, 28

drug companies and, 90–95

needed *vs.* received, 93

resistance to, 28

AIDS vaccine

funding for research on, 36

progress on, 32–37

Alliance 2015, 58

American Journal of Pathology, 98

Amoako, Julius, 81

Antiretroviral drugs (ARVs), 26–28

will curb African AIDS, 83–89

See also Highly active antiretroviral therapy

Army, U.S., 70

Asia, 42, 47, 49

Autoimmunity, 16

AZT (azidothymidine), 7–8, 28

personal experience with, 116